JAZZ LIVES

100 PORTRAITS IN JAZZ

JAZZ LIVES

GENE LEES

PHOTOGRAPHS BY JOHN REEVES

A FIREFLY BOOK

A FIREFLY BOOK

Cataloguing in Publication Data

Lees, Gene
  Jazz lives: one hundred portraits in jazz

Includes bibliographical references and index.
ISBN 1-895246-40-7

1. Jazz musicians.   I. Reeves, John, 1938-   .
II. Title.

ML3506.L44 1992   781.65'092   C92-094767-0

Published simultaneously in Canada by
Stewart House

Published in the United States by
Firefly Books (U.S.) Inc.
P.O. Box 1338
Ellicott Station
Buffalo, New York
14205

Printed and bound in Canada by Tri-Graphic Printing Ltd.

To the memory of Jeri Southern
1926-1991

Dizzy Gillespie
1917-1993

Contents

Some Words from the Photographer

Mum didn't understand it. Dad just plain hated it. I loved it.

I grew up in Canada at the western end of Lake Ontario. We lived in and around the then small town of Burlington. I was fifteen in 1955 and "it" was all that jazz that I had recently begun listening to. First I listened to radio broadcasts—Joe Rico's *Jump For Joe* which came from studios "high atop the beautiful Hotel Stuyvesant" in the heart of downtown Buffalo, New York, and Dick McDougall's *Jazz Unlimited* which originated from the studios of CJBC situated in what had once been a girl's school in the heart of downtown Toronto, Ontario. Next I began buying LPs and then as time went on I started to do a lot of my listening in the clubs and bars in and around Toronto and Hamilton, the two big towns in my part of the world. Listening convinced me that music is the greatest of the arts and that jazz is the greatest contemporary music, ergo the greatest contemporary art form.

Love of jazz centered my adolescent struggles to grow up and away from my parents' benign tyranny. Jazz became the music of my life and the men and women who played jazz became my idols. I've had a great life being John Reeves the photographer, but in an absolutely perfect world I would have chosen to be Zoot Sims or Mel Lewis or McCoy Tyner.

Confronting idols can be a tricky business. As I started this project I wondered if actual personalities would be able to sustain the burden of an admiration that's grown without any direct contact with them.

Apart from my psychological concerns there was a need to arrive at a photographic form for my meetings with these artists. I have for years been an admirer of the beautiful photojournalistic and "in-performance" work of shooters such as Milt Hinton, Herman Leonard and William Claxton, and I felt more than a little inadequate to pursue my jazz subjects by walking down their photographic trails. Finally I arrived at the "big face" portrait idea. I thought that straight intimate portraiture might yield viewers useful — and different — information that had not been provided in quite as much quantity as the other photographic approaches to jazz. Happily my years sojourning through Gene Lees' world of jazz threw me "smack dab in the middle" of the most altogether satisfactory group of people that I have ever encountered. What's more, my subjects seemed to relish just sitting and being themselves for the camera.

Somebody once said that there aren't any stupid jazz musicians because the music is too complex for a stupid person to play. That assertion proved to be astonishingly accurate. Again and again I found myself in the presence of musically gifted, intellectually vibrant, verbally articulate political and philosophical liberals. In the jazz culture the sexes, the races and the generations all play beautifully together. Jazz musicians take generous delight in each others' talents. They believe that the diligent pursuit of excellence leads to a more rewarding life and they want to believe that a free, sane, compassionate society may still be attainable.

Jazz Lives has been the greatest experience in my life as a photographer. My adolescent judgment has been vindicated. My love for the music continues to grow and the knowledge that there really is a community of gifted, thoughtful people out there provides precious reassurance as I contemplate the future in troubled times.

The good great American Dream is alive and well and living in the hearts of the world's jazz musicians.

John Reeves
Toronto, Canada
May 1992

The Tradition of Jazz

Everyone who loves jazz is aware that there is something in it that is somehow comforting, somehow healing. I suspect that this is because every once in a while, if only for a few bars or a chorus or two, or, when the groove is good, for as much as an hour, it takes us home to our lost garden, the eternal now.

The achievements of the system of thought bequeathed to us by the Greeks — observation, classification, skepticism, syllogism, induction, deduction — have been prodigious. Yet for all its achievements, almost everyone entrapped in it senses that there is something wrong with it, something that produces a feeling of being incomplete, of alienation.

Consciousness is a product of language. But the price we have paid for it is our separation from nature, the perpetual maddening flow of words through the mind, the unending observation of everything, including ourselves, the talking about existence rather than the direct experience of it.

The image of exile haunts the world's folklore. The myth of Adam and Eve and their expulsion from the garden for having partaken of the fruit of knowledge is one of the profound myths. We were expelled from nature the moment we learned to speak, to attach meanings to vocal noises, to make symbols of sounds. Verbalization, whether audible or silent in the mind, enabled us to visit the past and describe it and wander in speculation through the future. We escaped from now. And we rarely find our way home to it again. As a consequence of the spread of literacy, everyone in Western society is the prisoner of Greek reasoning. And few people understand the extent to which they are slaves of their own thought processes, which are in turn the direct consequence of the tyranny of language.

John 1:1: "In the beginning was the Word, and the Word was with God, and the Word was God." Again there is the emphasis on the importance of the word — the *logos* in Greek. In Genesis we find the story of the tower of Babel (Babylon). Adam's descendants, apparently not having learned how petulant and arbitrary the landlord could be, decided to build a tower to his abode, namely the heavens. For this impertinence he dispersed them and made them speak different languages so that they were now separated not only from nature but from each other. American slave-owners, who were nothing if not Bible-readers, applied the lesson of that story by mixing slaves of different languages so that they could not converse and therefore could not achieve the political cohesion necessary to co-ordinated rebellion. This caused Africans in America to forget their cultures and customs, and function as best they could in English, which they continue to this day to use with invention and poetry.

Jazz, through its rhythms and its difficult-to-define swing, sets up a hypnotic receptivity. Hypnosis is a process by which the conscious, rationalistic judgment is suspended, allowing the hypnotist directly to address the subconscious, which lacks the critical faculty and accepts whatever suggestion is made to it. Jazz, to a degree that depends on your ability or willingness to submit to it, gets you beyond the process of conscious judgment, of verbalizing, of observing yourself in the act of listening and thinking about your responses, which very act can make those responses evaporate. It opens, as it were, the doorway to the soul and gives the music direct access to the inner person. At the same time jazz combines a flowing rhythmic pulse with extraordinary emotional expressiveness and intellectual invention.

The removal of Africans to America occurred quite recently. In 1983, the Constitution of the United States was two hundred years old. The pianist and composer Eubie Blake was still alive; he turned one hundred that year, and died shortly after his birthday. He had personally lived through *half* the post-Revolutionary history of the United States.

In 1955, in Louisville, Kentucky, I interviewed on her 104th birthday a woman who had been born a slave and remembered the Civil War. The importation of slaves from Africa was not halted in the United States until 1808. Eubie Blake was born in 1883. He quite easily could have met someone who had been brought from Africa, and he assuredly could have known the sons or daughters of such people. That's how recent the connection to Africa is.

The African culture was primarily oral, and the very deprivation of formal literate education for blacks has had the effect of keeping a form of it alive well into our own time. An oral culture is inherently different from a literate one, since speech is a spontaneous and improvisational act. That there is a vocal quality about jazz instrumental music has always been recognized. In his 1971 book *Black Talk*, pianist and sociologist Ben Sidran wrote:

> The elements of black music most responsible for the impact it has are the vocalized tone and the peculiarly "black" approach to rhythm. These are essential elements of oral communication in general and allow for communication of a nonverbal nature, often at an unconscious level, to triumph over the rigid classification structure of any linguistic system and to continue in the face of cultural suppression. The vocalized approach is part of the greater oral ability to lend semantic significance to tonal elements of speech. Bornman has suggested that "while the whole European tradition strives for regularity — of pitch, of time, of timbre, and of vibrato — the African tradition strives precisely for the negation of these elements. In language, the African tradition aims at circumlocution rather than at exact definition. The direct statement is considered crude and unimaginative; the veiling of all content in ever-changing paraphrase is considered the criterion of intelligence and personality. In music, the same tendency toward obliquity and ellipsis is noticeable: no note is attacked straight; the voice or instrument always approaches it from above or below. The timbre is veiled and paraphrased by constantly changing vibrato, tremolo, and overtone effects."

In the liner notes for the famous Miles Davis *Kind of Blue* album (1959), the late Bill Evans wrote:

> There is a Japanese visual art in which the artist is forced to spontaneousness. He must paint on a thin stretched parchment with a special brush and black water, paint in such a way that an unnatural or interrupted stroke will destroy the line or break through the parchment. Erasures or changes are impossible. These artists must practice a particular discipline, that of allowing the idea to express itself in

communication with their hands in such a direct way that deliberation cannot interfere.

The resulting pictures lack the complex composition and textures of ordinary painting, but it is said that those who see well find something captured that escapes explanation. This conviction, that direct deed is the most meaningful reflection, I believe, has prompted the evolution of the extremely severe and unique disciplines of the jazz or improvising musician.

Though there have been major innovative white jazz musicians, such as Bix Beiderbecke on cornet, trombonist Jack Teagarden, and pianist Bill Evans, far the greater part of the inspiration and influence in jazz has come from black musicians. And the reason for this is not merely one of their early exposure to a highly rhythmic music.

A black child wishing to play jazz probably has an advantage over a white child with the same ambition, because he comes from a culture that places a value on spontaneity. He is psychologically more attuned to a music that requires that quality—although there are many black people whose upbringing has not inculcated this ideal in them. Indeed, an aspiration to white gentility destroyed it in many middle-class black families, and certainly in black universities. Nonetheless, it is generally true that those growing up in a black culture have tended to be infused with the value of spontaneity.

Jazz is black music not just because black musicians invented it but because to be jazz the music must be made in accordance with a tradition of spontaneity that is linked to an oral and sometimes even sub-verbal culture. However, since the days of its origins about one hundred years ago (and some would say less than that) it has spread to become not just a black musical language but an American musical language and, in the years since the Second World War, a universal one. There are superb jazz musicians from every country in the world, including Japan, whose formalized culture and rigid systems of training would seem to be hopelessly antithetical to the spirit and character of jazz.

It follows that those white cultures which (though to a lesser extent than the black culture) value spontaneity are likely to produce more jazz musicians than those that extol control and linear logic, as do the Germans and the English. These more spontaneous cultures include the Scots, the Irish, the Italians, and the Jews, and the preponderance of white jazz musicians comes from these groups and America's other minorities. This is as true in Canada as in the United States. The Anglo-Saxon jazz musician is a *rara avis*.

There is a theory that the samba of Brazil, in which the feet move only slightly while the body moves sensuously and joyously, was developed by a people dancing with their feet in chains. What kind of remarkable people could dance with feet in chains? Who would want to? Who would have a need to? A people, I would suggest, in touch with now.

The process by which someone from a culture that values restraint and the deliberate concealment of emotions — very English qualities — comes to play jazz, and for that matter to work in any of the performing arts, is bound to be different. He must overcome inhibitions that simply are not present, at least to the same degree, in someone from a culture that values display, flamboyance, overt expression. Early Celtic art was notably florid. And look at that mad Irish love of words, of soaring rhetoric and spontaneous public-house poetry. If it is no accident that many of the best jazz musicians in England are Celtic, neither is it an accident that so many of Britain's finest actors are also Celts, such as Alec Guinness, a Scot, Richard Burton, a Welshman, and Richard Harris, who is Irish. And look at how many playwrights (Sheridan, Wilde, Shaw, Synge) and poets and novelists the Irish and the Scots have given to the English language.

In earlier periods of European musical history, the creator of the music was himself a performer. As what we now call "classical" music evolved, this began to change. The first "classical" composers were very much involved in performance, and most were virtuosi and skilled improvisers. This continued through the eighteenth and well into the nineteenth centuries. Beethoven gave up improvising only when he became too deaf to hear himself. Chopin had a prodigious musical memory and his impromptus are apparently transcriptions of pieces he had earlier improvised. Perhaps if the recording process had been invented, he would have *written* far less than he did.

But a bifurcation grew gradually wider during the nineteenth century. The composer became king, the players merely vassals to his will. Thus the composer was separated from the performing and the performer from the creating of the music. An inevitable desiccation began to set in. Music moved toward being an exercise in logic and form, more "written," more "literate," if you will. In the twentieth century, this trend progressed toward disaster, and among those who consider themselves *cognoscenti* of classical music there is a certain condescension toward those composers whose music is accessible and overtly emotional, and a relegation of their work to a lower rank — Grieg, Tchaikovsky, Rachmaninoff.

It is significant, I think, that Rachmaninoff, whose music is intensely emotional and communicative, was one of the great virtuosi of the piano, and an improviser. Bill Evans once said to me, "Any music that is not in some way in touch with the process of improvisation is likely to be sterile."

A correlation between character and language will always be found. Descartes and Debussy could only have been French. Schoenberg, Schillinger, Webern could only have been German. And if the black culture puts a high value on spontaneity and the impulsive, the German culture places the highest value on *ordnung*, order. It is inevitable then that German composers would strive to develop orderly systems for making music, systems that eliminate as much as possible the variation and fallibility of human judgment, systems that free the composer of responsibility for his own acts, systems that would, after the work was completed, provide irrefutable justification for the way it was made and eliminate in turn the variability of the listener's response to it.

And though Debussy took ardent issue with the German dominance of classical music, its influence is still there. Thus twentieth-century classical music still is preoccupied with systems and logic for which the composer can be proclaimed brilliant, rather than with emotion. It has wandered farther and farther from what the Greeks thought was the purpose of tragedy (and in my opinion is the purpose of all art), namely catharsis, the freeing of the emotions by pity and terror.

It is axiomatic in all schools of psychology that repressed emotions fester, giving rise to any number of problems, from neurosis to ulcers to hysterical conversion to total mental collapse to murder. No one since Freud has seriously questioned this, except religious fundamentalists. And nothing has the capacity to release emotion like art, and no art like music, and no music like jazz.

It is an accident of circumstance, and a privilege, that I have met most of the major jazz musicians of our time and have known some of them very well; and since it is a young art, perhaps more than half of those who have ever lived. How old this music actually is depends on how you define it. If you accept that jazz as we know it is the lengthened shadow of trumpeter Louis Armstrong, whom I met a few times, then it has evolved in little more than my own lifetime. But if you date it from the time of the near-legendary New Orleans trumpet player Buddy Bolden and the great ragtime innovators, it is nearing the end of its first century. As my collaborator John Reeves puts it, "Jazz is even younger than photography."

I met John in the middle of a television talk show on which we were both guests. We have been friends ever since. We discovered quickly that we were born about fifteen miles apart, I in Hamilton and he in Burlington, Ontario, both of which are now in effect part of greater Toronto. We grew up in that part of Canada, and both attended (though at different times) the Ontario College of Art, I with the intention of being a painter, from which calling I was distracted by the siren songs of music and the printed page.

Jazz has had a profound effect on my own life, and my work. Jazz inculcated in me the value of the spontaneous, the thought caught and expressed in mid-flight. Alas, writing can be and indeed must be revised. You can't do that in jazz. Playing jazz is like painting on the wind.

I have been involved with jazz and jazz musicians from my early days. In time these people formed a large part of the population of my private world. Dizzy Gillespie, Oscar Peterson, Alan Broadbent, Phil Woods, Horace Silver, Benny Carter, and many more of the people in this book are friends of many years. Some of them, including Carmen McRae, have recorded my songs, and some of them, such as Roger Kellaway and Gerry Mulligan, have been my collaborators in the stringent craft of song-writing.

John, by contrast, knew few of these people personally. But he was a well-informed and perceptive lover of jazz, who selected this project as the next thing he wanted to do in life. I became his guide. I escorted him through my world, increasingly fascinated by his perceptions of these remarkable people as the proof sheets came up in the developer bath in his studio darkroom in Toronto.

The image of jazz musicians in my mind is at odds with much that has been written about them. Often you will see it said that they are inarticulate. I can only conclude that some of them did not feel like talking to the critic or the reporter who would author such a statement. They are, in fact, among the most articulate people I know, despite the shyness of some of them.

One thing especially struck me during the days of shooting, which went on from the summer of 1988 through to the spring of 1992: that jazz musicians are gentle and poetic people, on the whole. Another thing: despite the legend of the impoverished origins of jazz musicians (which was never true, with the notable exception of Louis Armstrong), they are for the most part solidly middle-class people from stable and educated homes. Almost all of them had staunch family support for the study of music. The movies have made much of junkie (Charlie Parker) or alcoholic (Red Nichols) jazz musicians eking out tortured lives, but as John and I went into the homes of jazz musicians day after day, I began to see that they were mostly happy people. As my late friend Paul Desmond (who alas is not in this book) put it, "If you can solve a few problems—hah! a few!—like finding some people to play with and getting somebody to pay you to do it, a jazz musician is just about the best thing in the world to be."

And they are very educated musicians, whether by dint of their own lonely studies of the textbooks or through formal university education. They are brilliant and thoughtful men and women. John has captured this truth here like no photographer I have ever seen. These are not photographs of musicians in transports of creativity, horn in mouth, grimacing with the effort. John caught them in private moods, in moments of repose or pensiveness or laughter. My regret is that we could not print all the thousands of pictures he shot, for they show each musician in this collection in his or her multiplicity of moods and fleeting expressions.

John and I decided to present the people in *Jazz Lives* chronologically, beginning with the music's oldest practitioners. The faces grow younger as you proceed through its pages and finally you realize that the rising generation of jazz players are the ones who are going to take this music into the twenty-first century. They are as diverse as the styles they create and embody, for jazz is nothing if not a celebration of the individual creative vision.

Gene Lees

JAZZ
LIVES

NEWELL (SPIEGLE) WILLCOX

Born: Cortland, New York, May 2, 1903

When John Reeves and I paid our visit to Spiegle Willcox in January of 1991 at his home near Cortland, New York, the trombonist almost certainly was the oldest jazz musician still performing, certainly the only prominent one. Newell Willcox, like most jazz musicians, and contrary to persistent legend, was born into the educated middle class. He was educated at Manlius Military School, near Syracuse, where he picked up the unexplained nickname Spiegle.

He made the decision to be a musician when he was fifteen, and worked his way up to playing in one of Paul Whiteman's orchestras. In late 1925, he joined the famous and highly influential Detroit orchestra headed by Jean Goldkette, the French-born, classically trained pianist and impresario. There Spiegle found himself sharing the bandstand with cornetist Bix Beiderbecke, saxophonist Frank Trumbauer, and trombonist Bill Rank.

In 1927, after his first son was born, Spiegle went home to Cortland and entered the family coal business, in which he worked for decades, though always playing for dancers on weekends. In 1975, violinist Joe Venuti dragged him back into jazz prominence with a Carnegie Hall reconstruction of the Goldkette band.

White-haired, witty, and cheerfully defiant of time, Spiegle stayed out there on the road, playing all over America and Europe with artists as varied as Romano Mussolini, Warren Vaché, and Canada's Climax Jazz Band. He lives in a big rustic house in the woods not far from Cincinnatus, which is in turn not too far from Cortland, where he was born. Now and then he sees his old friend Bill Challis, who wrote some of the very arrangements Spiegle played with Goldkette.

WILLIAM (BILL) CHALLIS

Born: Wilkes-Barre, Pennsylvania, July 8, 1904

Like Spiegle Willcox, Bill Challis has lived all his life near his birthplace. Challis played saxophone in Wilkes-Barre, performing—like Tommy and Jimmy Dorsey, Russ Morgan, and other natives of the Pennsylvania mining towns — for the dances of the miners and coal barons. Self-taught as an arranger, Challis wrote for a college band, which he eventually led, while he was a pre-law student at Bucknell University. He played in the Scranton Sirens, whose members included trumpeter Fuzzy Farrar and trombonist Russ Morgan, both of whom joined the Jean Goldkette band — the only one of Goldkette's many bands that bore his name. The others included the Casa Loma Orchestra, the antecedent of the white swing bands, and McKinney's Cotton Pickers, one of the inspirations of the black swing bands.

Bill's fellow Pennsylvanian, Fuzzy Farrar, a principal figure in the Goldkette band, brought both Spiegle Willcox and Bill Challis into its personnel. Challis wrote pioneering arrangements for the band, arrangements that were startling in their harmonic advancement. His big influence, Challis says, was Bix Beiderbecke. After the collapse of the Goldkette band for financial reasons, Challis joined Paul Whiteman and wrote still more music that featured Beiderbecke's cornet and Frank Trumbauer's saxophone. Like his friend Fletcher Henderson, for whose band he wrote a good deal, Challis was one of the principal architects of the Swing Era — one of those men who developed the

techniques of antiphonal writing for the trumpet, trombone, and saxophone sections. He continued to write through the era and afterwards, turning out beautifully crafted arrangements for the Casa Loma Orchestra, Artie Shaw, Charlie Barnet, and others.

Like Spiegle Willcox, Challis is proof that the jazz idiom was developed all over America, not just in New Orleans, Chicago, and New York. Living with his brother and sister-in-law in quiet retirement in Harvey's Lake, Pennsylvania — about twenty minutes' drive from Wilkes-Barre — Bill claims nothing for himself. But in recent years he has seen the importance of his work begin to be recognized.

4

ADOLPHUS ANTHONY (DOC) CHEATHAM

Born: Nashville, Tennessee, June 13, 1905

Doc Cheatham was known for much of his career as a fine lead trumpeter. One of the bands in which he filled that role was McKinney's Cotton Pickers, one of the stable of bands Jean Goldkette ran out of Detroit. Detroit has never been given its due as a cradle of jazz, nor for that matter has the Goldkette organization. Cheatham was with McKinney's Cotton Pickers (there was no one named McKinney) in 1931 and '32. Later he played with groups led by Cab Calloway, Teddy Wilson, and Benny Carter — another McKinney's alumnus.

When work was scarce in the jazz field, Doc played in Latin bands. His recognition as a jazz improviser came late in his life, and through the 1970s and eighties, he continued to work in small groups. He added singing to his bag of skills, performing songs with an ingratiating simplicity and then taking up the horn to deliver hot, big, soaring solos with a burnished tone in a style quite his own.

Through much of the 1980s and into the nineties, Doc fronted a group in Sunday matinees at the Sweet Basil club in New York, showing no diminution of abilities as he approached his ninetieth year. Indeed, most of Doc's best recordings have been made in his later years.

John Reeves saw something in Doc's face as he was shooting his portrait: the Indian quality, something which I had noticed some time before. While the African and European contributions to jazz are well documented, the contribution of musicians with Indian antecedents has been little noted. But then the mixture, through marriage, of African and native American blood lines has not been much noted either. Doc is classified as "black" under the inane system of ethnic designations still in effect in America. But take a good look at that face. It's Indian. Both of Doc's maternal grandparents were full-blooded Cherokee; his father's father was Choctaw. You will see more of the Indian presence in jazz in these pages.

6

BENNETT L. (BENNY) CARTER

Born: New York City, August 8, 1907

Benny Carter has been called "the gentleman of jazz," but no sobriquet can evoke the sheer elegance of the man or his music. From his pencil have come tunes as diverse as "Cow Cow Boogie" and "When Lights Are Low." Arranger, composer, pianist, saxophonist, trumpeter, Benny performs in all his capacities with discrimination and grace.

Carter was born a block from the acreage now occupied by Lincoln Center and educated at Wilberforce University, where he majored in theology. His mother was his first music teacher, but he was largely self-taught: in those days there were no jazz courses in high schools and universities. (Carter himself thinks in terms of *music*, and doesn't care for the undefinable term *jazz*.) He started with a C-melody sax, emulating Frank Trumbauer, and began writing early. "Bill Challis was my idol," he says. He met Challis when he was playing in Fletcher Henderson's band and Challis was writing for it. Then for a time Carter was music director of McKinney's Cotton Pickers. Another band he wrote for in the 1930s was that of Benny Goodman.

He lived in London for two years, leading a BBC staff band of American and British musicians. He returned to America in 1939 and led groups of his own, small ensembles and big bands. Carter became one of the first black musicians — not *the* first as that title is held by arranger and orchestrator Will Vodery — to penetrate the Hollywood studios. He wrote arrangements, usually for black singers such as Lena Horne appearing in white movies.

And he was instrumental in making the black and white musicians' union locals of Los Angeles into one. In the mid-1940s he returned to playing and travel, though he continued to write as well, turning out arrangements for most of the best singers of the 1960s. He continues to perform into the 1990s in vibrant good health, and lectures at Princeton and other universities. He now lives in an exclusive area of Los Angeles, drives a Rolls-Royce, and collects art.

Carter was one of my early idols, and one's early idols retain a permanent aura of magic.

Arthur Jacob Arshawsky (Artie Shaw)

Born: New York City, May 23, 1910

Three years after Benny Carter was born on the midtown West Side of New York City, Arthur Arshawsky was born on the Lower East Side. He grew up in New Haven, Connecticut, with his mother, feeling himself an outsider because his father had abandoned them — not the common thing in Jewish families. He learned early that he could make more money playing "Pony Boy" on a saxophone than he could at menial labor, and became a traveling musician. He took up clarinet, which was to become his principal instrument. For a time he worked in Cleveland as arranger and music director for the Austin Wylie dance band, traveling before he was twenty to Chicago to hear Louis Armstrong, who was to remain a lifelong idol. "Anyone born later," he has said, "cannot imagine the impact he had on all of us. Had Louis Armstrong never lived, there would no doubt be something called jazz, but it wouldn't be the same thing."

Shaw returned to his native city, New York, where for a time he shared a room with Bix Beiderbecke. He remembers listening to Debussy, Ravel, Stravinsky, and Dukas records with Bix. "I was trying to play like Bix on a saxophone." Shaw became a studio musician, working sometimes for a radio orchestra led by Bill Challis, and sometimes in a section with Benny Goodman, who would become his archrival. Benny Goodman's famous breakthrough success with a big band in 1935 had launched what would be called the Swing Era. Following this path, Shaw in 1937 formed a big band of his own, which became a huge success and established Shaw as a matinee idol. Later he wrote a book, *The Trouble with Cinderella*, about the psychological trauma of high public visibility, and he broke up his band in 1939, only to reform in 1940. He led a U.S. Navy band in the South Pacific during the Second World War, formed a new big band after a medical discharge, broke it, then started still another band in 1949. He broke that band up as well and performed with a small group, finally abandoning music as a profession in 1954 to pursue a dream of establishing himself as a writer.

Shaw is known almost as much for his marriages to famous beauties, Ava Gardner, Lana Turner, and Evelyn Keyes among them, as for his music. While Goodman was the consummate jazz clarinet technician, Shaw was considered by many musicians the richer, the more inventive and certainly the more lyrical player. And, unlike Goodman, Shaw welcomed the innovations of bebop, even incorporating some of its elements into his own playing. The quality of his work left admirers forever regretting that he gave up music.

Articulate, witty, bookish, Shaw has lived his later years in a solitary retirement in California, carefully guarding his musical legacy even as he claimed it was of little interest to him.

HARRY (SWEETS) EDISON

Born: Columbus, Ohio, October 10, 1915

The nickname came from Lester Young, whose language was original, piquant, and to the point. Sweets spent his childhood in Kentucky, where he was introduced to music by an uncle, the very man, Sweets says, from whom he derived his own lexicon of evocative expressions. ("He ain't worth four dead flies," Sweets said of somebody.) The question is: where did his uncle get these expressions?

The family moved back to Columbus, and in 1933, when he was eighteen, Sweets joined the Jeter-Pillars Orchestra in Cleveland, a few years after Artie Shaw had left that town. As a trumpet player, Sweets followed the inspiration of Louis Armstrong, though he early developed an approach of his own. He went with the band of Lucky Millinder, always an astute judge of musicians though he did not play an instrument himself, and then with Count Basie, for whom he wrote "Jive at Five," "Shorty George," and "Every Tub," as well as recording some memorable and very original solos.

Since the 1950s, Sweets has been a freelance musician, working with small groups of his own and co-leading one with saxophonist Eddie (Lockjaw) Davis. In the studios of Los Angeles he was what the musicians call a "first-call" player. Those laconic Harmon-muted solos on Frank Sinatra's records for Capitol and Reprise are the work either of Cappy Lewis or Sweets.

Sweets is one of those musicians who never stood still, incorporating many of the changes in jazz as they came along, including the innovations of bebop. Though a consummate technician, he favored a middle-register style long on melody and perceptive selectivity. There is a sense of inevitability, of rightness, about Sweets Edison solos.

PETER (PETE) RUGOLO

Born: San Piero, Sicily, December 25, 1915

A few years ago I ran into Pete Rugolo at a party. I told him of a night back in my home town, Hamilton, Ontario, when I went to hear one of the touring big bands I admired. I can still picture the scene: the old red-brick armory down on James Street North. I got into a conversation with the band's arranger. He was memorably kind to me, although I was very young and a stranger to him. He was already quite famous. We sat on the sidelines and discussed the music. He made me feel as if I mattered, and I never forgot him for it.

"Do you know who that man was?" I asked Pete at the party.

"No," Pete replied, looking quizzical.

"You. And I have meant to tell you about it for a long time."

Pete was born in Sicily, but was brought to America at a very young age. He became a student of expatriate French composer Darius Milhaud. While he was still in mil-

itary service, he sold an arrangement to Stan Kenton and, after the war, became the Kenton band's chief arranger. He was with Kenton from 1945 to 1949, which many people consider the band's glory years. It was Rugolo, along with Kenton, who discovered the high-flying horn of young Maynard Ferguson during a visit to Montreal. Pete's grand arrangements and compositions on the one hand embodied Kenton's ideas, and on the other shaped the character of the band. They featured passages of very wide voicings, and blazing brass played fortissimo. Though it became fashionable in later years to disparage the Kenton band, it did indeed expand the vocabulary of jazz orchestration, and it influenced generations of arrangers, particularly those who went into film scoring. There the dramatic musical vocabulary explored by Rugolo and Kenton proved particularly effective. Pete was one of the many composers with jazz experience to enter the field, and he wrote music for many films and television shows.

Gentle and self-effacing to a fault, Pete has had more influence on jazz than he would ever claim. He's also known for his cooking prowess, as gourmet Henry Mancini can attest, and his collection of fine wines and superior malt whiskey, as John Reeves can attest.

JOHN BIRKS (DIZZY) GILLESPIE

Born: Cheraw, South Carolina, October 21, 1917

No name blazes more brightly in the firmament of jazz than that of Dizzy Gillespie, as often as not called Birks by his friends, and the Sky King by Phil Woods. The last is a reference to Dizzy's unending travel: he seems always to be on a plane going somewhere, to some festival or concert in a far-off land.

It is almost banal to say that he is one of the major innovators. In tandem with his friend Charlie Parker, and in collaboration with other players such as saxophonist Don Byas and pianist Thelonious Monk, Birks revolutionized jazz in the 1940s through the development of bebop. The term was a humorous one, but unfortunate in that it trivialized the music and eased the way to disparagement from those critics who lacked the musical vocabulary to understand its harmonic, melodic, and rhythmic innovations.

Whoever was the primary innovator, Parker or Gillespie, it is beyond dispute that Dizzy was the great teacher, and one musician after another attests to his patience in explaining things to his juniors. Trumpet players particularly describe enlightening encounters with the grand guru of bop who, unlike Parker, lived to be an elder statesman and see their style of jazz spread throughout the world. But Dizzy's influence went far beyond the vocabulary of bebop. He was and is fascinated by all the music of the world, and brought into the jazz mainstream all sorts of Latin influences, from the Cuban to the Brazilian.

Dizzy came to his first prominence with the band of Cab Calloway and then played with Earl (Fatha) Hines, whose orchestra provided a warm home for those experimenting in search of a new vocabulary in jazz, Charlie Parker among them. By the mid-1940s, Dizzy had embraced the vocabulary developed by Parker and launched the bebop movement. After that he led a wild and highly original big band of his own. The Big Band Era was over, however, and Dizzy found it impossible to sustain this entourage. Thus Dizzy's most important work has been in the context of small groups.

He is a consummate leader. Aside from the depth of admiration musicians feel for him, there is probably no one in jazz as *loved* as Dizzy.

Like Spiegle Willcox, Dizzy doesn't remember who gave him his nickname. "But I'm glad he did," he says. The name refers to his incessant clowning: merely to be in his presence is cause enough to smile, if not laugh outright.

Dizzy lives—when he is not on a stage or an airplane—with his wife Lorraine in Englewood Cliffs, New Jersey. Dizzy could have been a dancer. Dizzy could have been a stand-up comedian, for he can make anything funny. But the work is always serious, for John Birks Gillespie is one of the authentic geniuses of twentieth-century music, an absolute original.

HENRY (HANK) JONES

Born: Vicksburg, Mississippi, July 31, 1918

Two major pianists, Oscar Peterson and André Previn, have told me that Hank Jones is their favorite pianist, and to make the statement more forceful, André added, "Regardless of idiom."

Like many another major jazz musician, Hank Jones might have become a "classical" musician had he not been black. I once heard Hank warming up on Chopin for a recording session, and was deeply impressed by his approach to that music. But black musicians did not aspire to concert careers when Hank was coming up — this was long before André Watts — and Hank became a jazz pianist, leading the way for two other musicians in the Jones family: the late Thad Jones, trumpeter and brilliant composer and arranger, and the remarkable drummer Elvin Jones.

Though he was born deep in the South, he grew up in Pontiac, Michigan, and seems to consider Michigan his home state. He was given solid musical training, but his father did not have it in mind that Hank should or would be a jazz musician. He gained his first experience in a church choir, and later played with regional bands, particularly in the Detroit area. When he went to New York in 1944, Hank heard the new music of Dizzy Gillespie and Charlie Parker, which he assimilated into his own playing. He was on a number of historic Charlie Parker recording dates.

Hank Jones is a particular favorite of other pianists, who admire his enormous but unprepossessing facility, his harmonic subtlety and sophistication, and his unfailing taste. He is a rich and sympathetic accompanist — he was Ella Fitzgerald's for several years — and an elegant soloist. He has played and recorded with almost everyone in jazz, including artists as varied as Milt Jackson, John Kirby, Howard McGhee, Coleman Hawkins, Julian (Cannonball) Adderley, Benny Goodman, and Artie Shaw. Indeed, he was a member of Shaw's last Gramercy Five group, and took part in Shaw's last recording session in 1954.

He tours the world constantly, though he has cut back on his New York studio work, preferring to spend his off time on his four-hundred-acre farm in upstate New York, not far from Cooperstown — always the impeccable jazz player, always in demand, admired and liked by everyone who has come into contact with his gentle humor and considerate warmth.

Hank wanted to farm that land, but his wife, Teddy, ever the realist, gave him a choice: "Do you want to be a farmer or a musician?

Music won. But the farm remains his refuge.

JAMES GEORGE (JIMMY) ROWLES

Born: Spokane, Washington, August 19, 1918

STACY ROWLES

Born: Los Angeles, California, September 11, 1955

Music runs in families; sometimes — as in the case of Bach, his antecedents, and his sons — for generations. Combinations of brothers, such as Zoot and Ray Sims and the three Jones brothers, are comparatively common. Pianist Jimmy and trumpeter Stacy Rowles are perhaps the only father-and-daughter combination of instrumentalists in jazz.

Nineteen days after Hank Jones was born in Vicksburg, Mississippi, Jimmy Rowles was born at almost the opposite corner of the United States — in Spokane, Washington. Eventually, Rowles became to Los Angeles what Hank was to New York, a highly admired jazz artist and first-call studio player with a refined touch and lovely tone. Like Hank, he was for a time Ella Fitzgerald's accompanist.

Jimmy's early reputation was built with the bands of Benny Goodman and, more significantly, Woody Herman. Settling in southern California, he worked in the recording studios and on film scoring: his lovely solos are heard, for example, in a number of Henry Mancini scores and albums. Jimmy has an antic sense of humor and has written a lot of sardonic songs, including "The Ballad of Thelonious Monk" and "The First American Gardener in Japan."

Jimmy and his wife have two daughters. One day when she was in junior high school, one of the daughters, Stacy, found two trumpets in the attic. She asked her father if he knew how to play them. Jimmy said he'd learned to play trumpet in the army, and showed her the embouchure.

After that, he said, she just could not leave the instrument alone, and soon joined the school band. In the 1980s, Stacy emerged as an outstanding jazz player, although she has not been able to make wide inroads into the Los Angeles studio world. "The pressure on a woman is there," Jimmy said. "The discrimination against her because she's a woman is subtle, but it's there."

Stacy's career in jazz flourished, however, and she continued recording and touring. The pianist on many of her dates was one of the finest in the business: her father. And his pride in her is obvious. You just have to look at John Reeves' pictures.

GREIG STEWART (CHUBBY) JACKSON
Born: New York City, October 25, 1918

DUFF CLARK (DUFFY) JACKSON
Born: Freeport, Long Island, New York, July 3, 1953

The band that clarinetist Woody Herman had developed by the start of 1945, later known as the First Herd, looked forward, not back. It embraced the innovations of Dizzy Gillespie (who had written for Woody as early as 1942) and Charlie Parker. With the approaching end of the Second World War, it embodied an ebullience that was almost Dadaesque in its irreverence and mocking laughter. Titles were wild ("Your Father's Mustache") and silly ("Goosey Gander") and exultant ("Blowin' Up a Storm"). The driving spirit of that band was bassist Chubby Jackson, who, with a perpetual huge grin, urged the band on with cries of "Go-go-go!" Without him, it would have been a superb band; with him, it was a truly great band.

Chubby had worked with bands of the cornier persuasion, including those of Johnny Messner, Jan Savitt, and Henry Busse. But he really began to grow during his stay from 1941 to 1943. Chubby with Charlie Barnet found his best showcase with Herman, however, between 1943 and '46. After that, he led his own groups, worked with Charlie Ventura's small band, and, with his flair for comedy and his outgoing personality, was the host of a popular children's television show for a number of years.

Chubby's son Duffy started studying drums at the age of four with Don Lamond, one of the fixtures of that First Herd. Duffy was a working musician when he was hardly into his teens. Later he played with a quintet led by Milt Jackson and Ray Brown. Then he worked with trombonist Kai Winding, Terry Gibbs (another Herman alumnus), and finally with Woody himself. He toured with Benny Carter, Lena Horne, and Sammy Davis Jr. Eventually Duffy became the drummer with the Count Basie band, a singular honor: no band in history was ever held in higher regard for sustained and effortless swing.

The Jacksons live in California. Now and then, Duffy works with his father. They make an exuberant pair, and laughter is never far away.

JOSEPH GOREED (JOE WILLIAMS)

Born: Cordele, Georgia, December 12, 1918

Joe Williams is one of the great bass-baritone singers of our time. He astounds me every time I hear him: the range and flexibility of his voice, his utter control of it, the depth of its passion. Joe is known as a blues singer, and he is a great one, but he is also one of the most sensitive ballad singers ever to grace popular music. And I have never heard a singer swing a band the way Joe can.

He grew up in Chicago, where he experienced severe discrimination, and not only from whites. Within the black community, the ideal was what Joe called "light-skinned pretty boys." He once said, "My light-skinned black brothers really whipped a racist color game on me." As handsome and imposing as he is, he was,

he says, at least twenty-five before he was "comfortable with my blackness."

Joe is very much a product of the rich Chicago jazz tradition. He gained his early experience in that city, working with bands led by clarinetist Jimmie Noone and pianist and organist Tiny Parham. In 1943, he joined Lionel Hampton's band at the minuscule (even for those days) salary of eleven dollars a night. Through the 1940s, he worked various bands, never getting the recognition he deserved. He worked briefly with Count Basie in 1950. Then, in 1954, he rejoined Basie and recorded Memphis Slim's "Every Day I Have the Blues." It brought him the stardom that had eluded him for twenty years. With wry humor, he quotes Duke Ellington: "They don't want you to get famous too young. You might get a chance to enjoy it."

But Joe did get a chance to enjoy it. Nearly forty years after "Every Day" became a hit, he was still singing it, still exercising that great, glorious, incomparable voice.

MARIAN MARGARET (TURNER) MCPARTLAND

Born: Windsor, England, March 20, 1920

The world of jazz is interwoven with delicate threads of relationships.

The cornetist Jimmy McPartland was part of a circle of young musicians who were learning to play jazz in Chicago in the 1920s under the inspiration of Louis Armstrong and Bix Beiderbecke. Indeed, in 1924, when Jimmy was only seventeen, he replaced Beiderbecke in the Wolverines, an all-white Chicago-based group inspired by the New Orleans Rhythm Kings. During the Second World War, McPartland was posted to Europe. In Belgium, he met a young English pianist named Marian Turner who, like McPartland, was entertaining British and American troops.

The young woman's training was entirely in classical music. Through Jimmy she became aware of jazz, and with his encouragement attempted to play it. They were married and in 1946 he took her home to the United States, where she struggled to overcome the condescension of musicians toward women (not to mention non-Americans) who tried to play jazz. At first Marian worked with Jimmy's group. It was at that time that I first met her and we became friends. She was the first European jazz musician I ever knew. We in North America were not really aware of how the music had spread beyond the borders of its homeland.

By 1950, Marian was leading her own trio at the Hickory House in New York. Gradually musicians began to take her seriously, and she was instrumental in developing the careers of any number of young artists just making their mark. In the years since, she has become not only respected but highly admired as a pianist who keeps on growing and evolving, and a teacher and fervent missionary of the music.

She and Jimmy eventually divorced, yet remained friends. Early in 1991, when Jimmy was dying, she asked me: "Do you think Jimmy and I should remarry?" Without a second thought I said "Yes." But there wasn't time.

Marian is a pioneer who, along with fellow pianist Mary Lou Williams and a few more, blazed the trail for all the younger women jazz players who have followed.

THE MODERN JAZZ QUARTET

JOHN AARON LEWIS
Born: La Grange, Missouri, May 3, 1920

MILTON (MILT) JACKSON
Born: Detroit, Michigan, January 1, 1923

PERCY HEATH, JR.
Born: Wilmington, North Carolina, April 30, 1923

CONRAD HENRY KIRNON (CONNIE KAY)
Born: Tuckahoe, New York, April 27, 1927

In its early years — its prototype was founded in 1946—the Modern Jazz Quartet included bassist Ray Brown and drummer Kenny Clarke. By 1955, they had been replaced, respectively, by Percy Heath and Connie Kay. Though there have been periods of hiatus when its four distinctive players went their separate ways, the group has never really disbanded. It has had the same personnel since Connie Kay's arrival in 1955. Thus it has existed longer than any group in the history of jazz.

The MJQ, as it is universally known, is an incredible delight to listen to. John Lewis (opposite top left), the scholarly, soft-spoken, diffident music director of the group, plays what sounds like a simple style of piano. Be not deceived. His colleague Milt Jackson reigns as the most powerful voice on vibraharp in jazz, with a bluesy style and chromatic fluency that prompted someone to dub him the Steel Bender. John accompanies him in a spare, delicate counterpoint rather than the chordal style common to bebop. Sometimes John will play, say, two or three select notes behind a passage. They are the perfect two or three notes, expressions of the man's exquisite taste and unfaltering musicality. Percy Heath (top right) is a powerfully rhythmic bassist, again one of those players who produces exactly the right notes. Connie Kay's style on drums is unlike that of anyone else: you can recognize it on a record immediately. It is a rather soft style, and he has a way of setting up an almost lacey sound with brushes on cymbal that, for all its delicacy, swings strongly.

John is a product of the American West. He grew up in New Mexico, where his ancestors on both sides trace their histories back generations: Comanche on one side, Cherokee on the other. This heritage is one reason he took a double major at the University of New Mexico — anthropology and music. After the Second World War, while he was writing for and playing in Dizzy Gillespie's big band, John took his doctorate in music at the Manhattan School of Music.

Milt Jackson (bottom left)—known universally as Bags — was the first bebop vibraphonist. He first worked with John Lewis in the Dizzy Gillespie big band.

Jazz often runs in families, and Percy Heath has famous musical brothers: saxophonist Jimmy and drummer Albert, nicknamed Tootie. Before becoming a professional musician, Percy was a fighter pilot.

Self-effacing Connie Kay (bottom right) almost never plays solos. But his generous support of others brings out their best. When I mentioned to John Lewis that Connie was Paul Desmond's favorite drummer, he said with his usual diffidence, "Mine too."

They are a remarkable ensemble with an almost telepathic rapport. The MJQ was original from the moment of its foundation, and it still is.

DAVID WARREN (DAVE) BRUBECK

Born: Concord, California, December 6, 1920

When the Dave Brubeck Quartet first became popular in 1951, the press made much of the fact that Dave had studied classical music. Since the earliest days of jazz, most jazz musicians, contrary to myth, have. But Dave was made to look like a sort of oddity, an aloof jazz intellectual, when he is anything but that. Dave's father was a champion rodeo rider who managed a 45,000-acre cattle ranch north of Stockton, California. He wanted his sons to follow in his footsteps: Dave, for one, was roping steers by the time he was fourteen.

Dave does not know the full story of the family's Indian background, only that it is there. His mother suppressed it. His father would start to talk about it, saying that his boys should be proud of their heritage, and she would cut him off with "Why are you telling them this nonsense?"

She was a pianist, and Dave's first teacher. She encouraged music in her sons, and Dave went off to study music at the College of the Pacific in Stockton. The Canadian-born composer Gil Evans, one of the most influential musicians in jazz history, grew up in Stockton; Dave's brother Henry, a drummer, played with Evans there. Later Dave studied composition at Mills College with Darius Milhaud, after whom he named one of his sons. Another son, Dan, is the drummer for the jazz band The Dolphins.

Dave's association with alto saxophonist Paul Desmond was one of the most successful in jazz history: the Dave Brubeck Quartet turned out an enormous body of memorable recordings between 1951 and 1967, when Dave disbanded it to write and Paul went solo. The group attained such popularity that Dave became one of the small body of jazzmen to make the cover of *Time* magazine. A tune Desmond wrote for the quartet, "Take Five," became the first million-seller record in jazz history. It was one of many experiments the group made with unconventional time-signatures, yet for all his popularity, Dave has never been given adequate credit for his contribution to leading jazz away from a relentless four-four time.

He and Paul could not have been more unlike: Paul the urbane, irresponsible, charming womanizer, Dave the solid, gentle, faithful family man, raising five boys, all of whom have become musicians. Darius teaches music at a black university in South Africa, ironically a part-Indian American apostle of jazz to the Africans.

Dave, who views himself primarily as a composer who plays piano, has written some excellent music in the form of ballets, cantatas, an oratorio, orchestral works, and piano pieces, but he will probably always be best remembered for that great quartet with Desmond. Once after a concert we fell to reminiscing about Paul. "I still miss him, Dave," I said.

"Oh boy," Dave said with a sigh, "so do I."

CLARK TERRY

Born: St. Louis, Missouri, December 14, 1920

Say "C.T." in the jazz world and everyone knows who you mean. There is only one C.T. He is not only one of my favorite trumpet players, he is one of my favorite people: warm, laughing, loving, and funny.

Clark Terry grew up in deep poverty in St. Louis. Even as a little boy he wanted to play the trumpet, but since the family could not afford one, he made an imitation instrument out of a piece of garden hose that he wired into a coil. He put a funnel in one end for a bell. He was able to produce so much sound on the thing that neighbors, whether in self-defense or compassion or both, finally bought him a real trumpet.

Clark's command of the instrument, and of fluegelhorn, is awesome. And sometimes, just for fun, he will "trade fours" with himself, four-bar phrases alternating on the two horns, with one horn held and fingered by the left hand. That is for laughter. But Clark's playing is serious, full toned, rich, inflective, beautiful, swinging, and unmistakable: you can detect him in two bars. Sometimes in a single note. And this is in an incredible variety of contexts: he has recorded with everyone you could ever think of, including Duke Ellington, Gerry Mulligan, Bob Brookmeyer, Zoot Sims, and Joe Venuti.

He is, as well, the most inventively humorous scat singer I've ever heard. His "lyrics" tread to the edge of the salacious, then decay into the incomprehensible. This practice has earned him the nickname Mumbles.

Once, when he was very young, work-ing in a circus band, Clark and a fellow musician were chased by a white mob in Jacksonville, Florida. They ran into a construction site and buried themselves in mud, listening to the mob as it ran among the piles of lumber looking for them. How much our world would have been diminished had their pursuers found them; and we would never know. Doubtless we have suffered countless such losses, and do not know. That Clark is filled not with rage but with humor, and that he so loves his fellow man, is one of the greatest triumphs of the human spirit. Straight ahead, C.T.

WILLIAM (BILLY) TAYLOR

Born: Greenville, North Carolina, July 24, 1921

Pianist and composer Billy Taylor was probably the first man to call jazz America's classical music. Like many jazz musicians, Billy is a product of the educated middle class. He is the son of a dentist, like Miles Davis. His mother was a school teacher. Billy enrolled at Virginia State College as a sociology major but switched to music, graduating in 1942. His doctorate came in 1975 from the University of Massachusetts. He has honorary degrees from six universities, and he is a Duke Ellington Fellow at Yale.

Billy founded the Jazzmobile more than twenty-five years ago, bringing free jazz concerts to the streets of New York City and offering clinics and workshops. In addition, Billy has been active as a television personality, doing reports every month or so on important jazz figures for *CBS Sunday Morning*. Before that, he was music director of *The David Frost Show*, the first black musician to hold such a position in network television. Because of such activities, Stan Kenton commented shortly before his death in 1980 that Billy was the most important living figure in jazz.

With his knowledge of history, musical and otherwise, Billy quietly rejects the image of the early jazzman as an uneducated autodidact, creating the music out of thin air and natural instinct—which he calls with a wry smile the "noble savage" theory of jazz genesis.

Effective teacher and evangelist for the music though he may be, Billy is first of all a pianist and composer. He has worked with Ben Webster, Dizzy Gillespie, Charlie Parker, Eddie South, Stuff Smith, Roy Eldridge, Don Redman, and countless more. Of his own crystalline, contrapuntal, light boppish style, he says that it is rooted in Art Tatum, Fats Waller, Debussy, Ravel, Bach, Ben Webster, and Eddie South.

Jazz, Billy says, "is an international music. It comes from the black experience, but one of the strengths of that experience is that it can be appropriated by people who don't belong to that ethnic group. All of my career, because I am black, it has been assumed that I think only blacks can play jazz. And I don't think that."

HERBERT GEORGE (HERB) ELLIS

Born: Farmersville, Texas, August 4, 1921

RAYMOND MATTHEWS (RAY) BROWN

Born: Pittsburgh, Pennsylvania, October 13, 1926

There are few closer friendships in the jazz world than that of guitarist Herb Ellis and bassist Ray Brown. They have been roommates, golf partners, and pranksters together for many years. From 1953 until 1958 they constituted two-thirds of the Oscar Peterson Trio. Once as a prank Ray dyed his hair flaming red and Herb dyed his black. Oscar pretended not to notice.

Herb studied from 1941 to 1943 at North Texas State University, where his classmates included saxophonist Jimmy Giuffre and composer Gene Roland. They were among the first jazz musicians to be trained at that university, which later became one of the foremost jazz education institutes in America. There he was introduced to the playing of guitarist Charlie Christian, whose work formed the foundation of Herb's style. He dropped out before graduation to go with the Russ Morgan band, then joined Glen Gray and the Casa Loma Orchestra, and, eventually, Jimmy Dorsey. That rhythm section included bassist John Frigo and pianist Lou Carter; along with Herb, they left Dorsey to form a trio called the Soft Winds. The new trio was far ahead of its time. Ray Brown, who was already with Oscar Peterson, heard Herb with the Soft Winds, and recommended him to Oscar, who hired him.

Ray, on his arrival in New York in 1945, had looked up his friend Milt Jackson. Jackson introduced him that very evening to Dizzy Gillespie. "You want a gig?" Dizzy asked. He hired him on the spot. Ray has never looked back. He instantly became an important figure in the jazz world, with his powerful pulse and big sound. When Jackson formed the Milt Jackson Quartet (note the initials: MJQ), Ray was its bassist, John Lewis the pianist, and Kenny Clarke the drummer. After Ray was replaced by Percy Heath, the group was renamed (with the same initials) the Modern Jazz Quartet. In the meantime Ray teamed up with Oscar Peterson in a history-making duo, which expanded into a trio with guitarist Barney Kessel and later Herb Ellis.

Ray is one of the seminal players in jazz history. His approach to the bass — "My heart is in that sound," he once told me — has made him one of the most influential figures in its evolution as a jazz instrument.

When Herb and Ray were with Oscar, they would practice all day, trying out, as Oscar put it, "all the possibles." All the possible ways to go through the chord changes and see if they could throw Oscar off-stride that evening.

There has never been a tighter trio in jazz, and as the 1990s dawned, Herb and Ray were periodically out on the road again with Oscar — still playing golf, still playing their practical jokes.

JACKIE AND ROY
ROY JOSEPH KRAL

Born: Chicago, Illinois, October 10, 1921

JACQUELINE RUTH (JACKIE) CAIN

Born: Milwaukee, Wisconsin, May 22, 1928

When pianist Roy Kral was in his teens, he approached Ralph Capone, brother of the world's most famous gangster, and said he wanted to start a band. Ralph Capone told him to put a band together and audition for him. Capone subsequently hired him for one of his clubs. That's the way it was in Chicago in the twenties and thirties: "the boys" controlled the nightclubs.

Chicago is the hub of the jazz world in the U.S. middle west: the talent of the nearby cities usually goes first to Chicago, not New York. And in 1947, a strikingly pretty and gifted young singer named Jackie Cain came down to Chicago from Milwaukee and met Roy. They sang in a quartet at a club called Jump Town. Early in 1948, they joined Charlie Ventura's Bop for the People. Their recordings with that group, including "Lullaby in Rhythm," exposed them to a national jazz audience. Soon they had their own TV show in Chicago. They were married in June 1949.

From then until now, they have been major stars in jazz, singing hip, cool, beboppish unison lines accompanied by a rhythm section whose central figure is Roy on piano. For years one of Jackie's closest friends was another gifted singer, Roy's sister Irene. All three, Jackie, Roy, and Irene, became like family to me. We lost Irene to cancer in 1978.

Jackie and Roy later began writing and singing jingles for television commercials. This is a jealously guarded field, with those who are already in it anxious to keep everybody else out, for the reason that it is enormously lucrative. The money they earned in television, far more than their records, bought them their handsome three-storey home on a leafy street in Montclair, New Jersey, from which on a clear day they can see the towers of Manhattan.

There is one thing strange about Jackie and Roy: they never seem to age. They go on year after year delighting their audiences and inspiring their friends. Jackie describes Roy as "my colleague, my lover, and my friend." They are as harmonious in their life together as they are in their music.

CARMEN MCRAE

Born: New York City, April 4, 1922

Carmen McRae is the true *grande dame* of jazz. Like so many of the best women jazz singers, including her friends Shirley Horn and the late Sarah Vaughan, Carmen is an accomplished pianist. This means she not only has a feeling for harmony, she has true knowledge of it. Carmen always knows exactly what she is doing.

The term *jazz singer* is a dubious one, and Sarah Vaughan objected to it. It means many things to many people, including merely a style that entails a certain indefinable jazz feeling. If it means anything specific, it surely denotes someone who can improvise with the voice. In a well-made song, the intervals of the music bear a significant relationship to the natural inflections of the words, and to alter the melody compromises the meaning and diminishes the dramatic effect of the song as a whole. Unfortunately, that is exactly what all too many "jazz singers" do. Carmen is a spectacular exception. When she changes the melodic intervals, she somehow, mysteriously, deepens the song, increasing the impact of the words.

Carmen began her singing career in 1944 with Benny Carter's orchestra. She sang with Count Basie, then became an intermission pianist and singer at Minton's Playhouse, the Harlem club known as the cradle of bebop. Her recording career began comparatively late, in 1954, when she was thirty-two. It has never ceased, and in 1990 she recorded an album in tribute to Sarah Vaughan.

Married twice, to drummer Kenny Clarke and trumpeter Ike Isaacs, both now dead, she now lives alone in Los Angeles on "Summit Ridge Drive," made famous as the title of a hit by Artie Shaw's Gramercy Five. Prickly, proud, defiant, irreverent, and charmingly funny when she wants to be, Carmen is one of the greatest singers jazz has ever produced. A striking beauty in her youth, she now seems like a queen gazing absently into the mysteries of her own storied past.

MUNDELL LOWE

Born: Laurel, Mississippi, April 21, 1922

Guitarist Mundell Lowe has performed in a notable variety of styles and idioms. From 1936, when he was fourteen, until 1940, he played traditional New Orleans jazz in that city, at a time when many of its founding figures were still around. Then he went to Nashville and played what was then known as hillbilly music, later refined to country and western, performing on *Grand Ol' Opry* radio broadcasts. He went with the Jan Savitt band in 1942, then into the U.S. Army. On being discharged in 1945, he joined the Ray McKinley band and stayed for two years. Somewhere along the way, he — like Herb Ellis and just about every other guitarist in jazz — came under the influence of Charlie Christian, and then in the period of bop evolution, of Jimmy Raney.

Mundy, as he is known to friends, then played in small groups led by Mary Lou Williams, Red Norvo, and Ellis Larkins while studying composition with Hall Overton, working on staff at NBC, and even doing some off-Broadway acting. He formed a quartet that included Red Mitchell on bass, and while working with Mitchell in New Orleans discovered and hired a pianist from New Jersey who was then a student at Southeastern Louisiana University — Bill Evans. Mundy Lowe was Bill's first champion in the business.

Mundy was a member of the Sauter-Finegan Orchestra in 1952 and '53, and in 1952 began working with Benny Goodman. He played with Goodman intermittently until 1984.

In 1965 Mundy moved to Los Angeles, where he worked mostly as a film and television composer. In 1983 he became music director of the Monterey Jazz Festival. All the while he continued to perform in his polished, thoughtful, unassuming style, touring from time to time with Benny Carter. He also toured with his gifted wife, singer Betty Bennett. He speaks pretty much as he plays, softly and with a sound of the South.

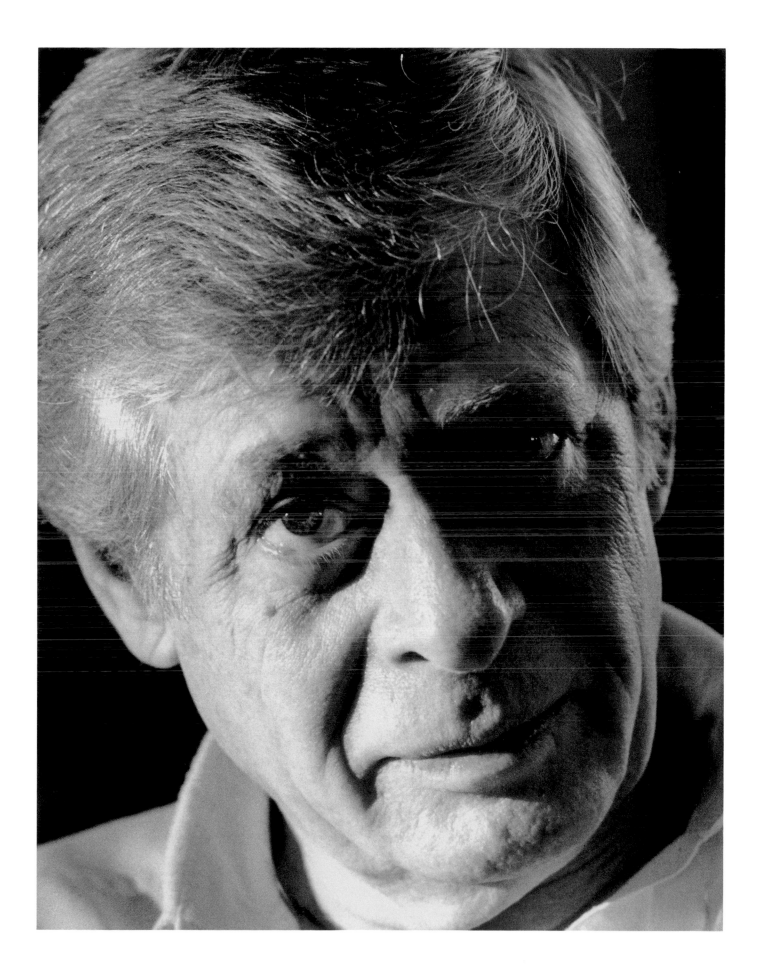

RALPH BURNS

Born: Newton, Massachusetts, June 29, 1922

In the 1940s, certain arrangers were associated with certain bands, just as certain baseball and hockey players were linked as if by predestination with certain teams. Sy Oliver wrote for Tommy Dorsey, though he had written for other bands; Jerry Gray wrote for Glenn Miller, though he had previously written for Artie Shaw. One of the strongest relationships was that of Ralph Burns to the Woody Herman band. Woody used to say, "I'm just an editor," but this self-deprecation could not hide the fact he was one of the great editors. And he always said that Ralph Burns gave him the courage to change arrangements. Burns in turn found in Herman and the Herman band the perfect vehicle for his outstanding talent as a writer.

Ralph entered the New England Conservatory of Music in 1938, when he was sixteen, studied there through 1939, then wrote for the band of Charlie Barnet. He joined Woody Herman as pianist and arranger in 1944, becoming a star of that organization along with trumpeter Pete Candoli, drummer Dave Tough, bassist Chubby Jackson, saxophonist Flip Phillips, and trombonist Bill Harris. He was thus the main arranger during the transition from the so-called Band that Plays the Blues to the Herd that recorded "Caldonia," "Wild Root," "Northwest Passage," "Happiness Is Just a Thing Called Joe," and others in a long list of mid-1940s hits. The Second World War was ending, and the band had an exuberance that made it one of the most exciting bands in history. Ralph Burns was one of the musi-

cians who gave it that spirit. Burns' compositions for Herman included "Apple Honey," "Bijou," and "Lady McGowan's Dream." Particularly interesting was a three-part Burns composition called *Summer Sequence*, to which he later wrote an addendum titled *Early Autumn*, which made Stan Getz a tenor saxophone star.

Burns stopped playing with the band in 1945, but continued to write for it. Gradually he became known as an arranger and orchestrator of Broadway shows, and later of Hollywood film scores. His friendship with Herman continued until Woody's death in 1987.

MELVIN EPSTEIN (MEL POWELL)

Born: New York City, February 12, 1923

Benny Goodman was not noted, shall we say, for avuncular solicitude toward the musicians and singers who worked for him. When Peggy Lee joined his band in July 1941, he gave her no rehearsal time to learn arrangements written for another singer, Helen Forrest. Peggy's salvation was the Goodman band's eighteen-year-old pianist, Mel Powell, who led her through them.

Mel Powell wrote an amazing chapter in jazz history, considering how little time he spent in the jazz world. A child prodigy classical pianist who had his own Dixieland jazz group at twelve, he joined Goodman just before Peggy did. He was not only a remarkable pianist, he quickly established himself as an enormously gifted arranger and composer, with such pieces of his own as "Mission to Moscow," "Clarinade," and "The Earl," and arrangements on "Jersey Bounce" and "Darktown Strutter's Ball". Bored with playing the same material night after night, Mel left Goodman in the summer of 1942 and went to England and France in the Army Air Force orchestra of Major Glenn Miller. He returned at war's end to a promising recording career which he gradually abandoned to his studies with Paul Hindemith at Yale. When Hindemith returned to Europe to live, Mel became a full professor of composition, then head of the Yale composition department. He turned out a small body of increasingly challenging exploratory "classical" music that even his friend André Previn found hard to understand.

Eventually Mel moved to California to head the composition department of the California Institute for the Arts. And then suddenly, in 1987, after repeated entreaties by his wife, the actress Martha Scott, and various friends, he returned to the jazz world to perform and record at a floating jazz festival on the S.S. *Norway*. The album proved him to be as fleet and interesting a pianist as he had been in his youth. In the spring of 1990, the Los Angeles Philharmonic performed Mel's concerto for two pianos, for which he was awarded a Pulitzer Prize.

Early in the 1980s, Mel noticed the onset of a neurological disorder that eventually confined him to an electric wheelchair. This did nothing to diminish his passion for life and music, nor his wit, his laughter, and his many friendships. He is an astonishingly brilliant man whose name still echoes in the jazz world he so briefly inhabited. His recordings, with Goodman and on his own, remain as fresh as when they were made.

WALTER JOSEPH (PETE) CANDOLI
Born: Mishawaka, Indiana, June 28, 1923

SECONDO (CONTE) CANDOLI
Born: Mishawaka, Indiana, July 12, 1927

Pete (left in photos) and Conte Candoli would be high on anyone's list of illustrious brothers in jazz. Both came to the fore in the exuberant First Herd of Woody Herman, the band that included Ralph Burns and trombonist Bill Harris. Pete had played in the bands of Sonny Dunham, Will Bradley, Ray McKinley, Tommy Dorsey, and Teddy Powell, but it was Herman who featured him to fullest advantage. Because he was so handsome and so powerful a trumpet player, Pete took on a Superman status, and finally Woody featured him in that role. In a Superman costume made by his wife, Pete would leap onstage from the wings, trumpet held high, and blast out the high notes. It was very funny, and typical of that brilliant, crazy band.

Conte Candoli first played with Woody in 1943 during the summer vacation months, when he was still a sixteen-year-old high school student. On graduation in 1945, he joined the band full-time, where the brothers Candoli sat side by side in the trumpet section.

Pete is primarily a lead-trumpet player. Rob McConnell has said, "Give me a great drummer and a great lead trumpet and I'll give you a great band." The lead-trumpet chair is a strenuous and demanding position. Pete is one of the best.

After leaving Woody, Pete played lead for Boyd Raeburn, Tex Beneke, Jerry Gray, Les Brown, and Stan Kenton. He settled in Southern California and immediately found himself in demand in the studios. If you ever see the Marlon Brando film *One-Eyed Jacks*, note the solo trumpet in Hugo Friedhofer's haunting score. That's Pete.

Conte is a bebopper inspired by Dizzy Gillespie. He has played with so many major jazz performers that it is impossible to list them all. Gerry Mulligan, Teddy Edwards, Shelly Manne, Terry Gibbs are only a few. Like many jazz musicians, Conte is active as a teacher.

From time to time, Conte and Pete perform together. You can hear the differences in their playing. And you can notice the warm fraternal love they have for each other, which John Reeves has captured so well in these portraits.

MAXWELL (MAX) ROACH

Born: New Land, North Carolina, January 10, 1924

"Think," bassist Bill Crow says, "of all the drummers who quit playing when they first heard Max Roach." Excepting Kenny Clarke, no one else had as much to do with the transition from swing-band drums to the newer, more flexible, more polyrhythmic style called for by bebop. Max was a major innovator.

Though he was born in North Carolina, Max grew up in Brooklyn, a prolific incubator of jazz musicians. He began playing drums in gospel bands when he was ten, and later studied at the Manhattan School of Music. When he was eighteen, he began a propitious association with Dizzy Gillespie and Charlie Parker, taking part in the famous jam sessions at Minton's Playhouse in Harlem where the young boppers polished their craft and separated the men from the boys. Only master musicians were able to keep up with their daring harmonic and rhythmic explorations. Max was one of those who did. He recorded frequently with Gillespie and Parker and then became associated with the new kid in town, one Miles Dewey Davis. Max recorded with the Miles Davis nonet, a group that included John Lewis and Gerry Mulligan. It grew out of the innovations that Gil Evans had brought to the Claude Thornhill band. The resulting Capitol album was eventually issued under the title *Birth of the Cool*. Later, Max led a quartet with the brilliant and tragically short-lived trumpeter Clifford Brown.

Sensitive and reflective, Max was particularly tortured by racism, and became an outspoken activist against it. Much of his work from the 1960s on has expressed his feelings on racial matters. He has remained an innovator, working in the field of so-called free jazz with such players as Anthony Braxton and Cecil Taylor. Max has also become an important composer for film and theater and a prominent educator, lecturing on music at the University of Massachusetts at Amherst and other schools.

Max makes a fascinating point about jazz drums. He notes that only in America did drummers start playing with the feet as well as the hands. What jazz drummers have achieved in developing the independence of all four limbs of the body is amazing, and none is more amazing than Max.

Oh yes, one more thing: Max Roach is one of the handsomest men I've ever met.

Milton M. Rajonsky (Shorty Rogers)

Born: Great Barrington, Massachusetts, April 14, 1924

One of the most important training grounds in the arts is New York City's High School of Music and Arts, whose famous alumni are legion and legend. Among them is trumpeter and composer Shorty Rogers, one of the most distinctive soloists to come up through the 1945 band of Woody Herman. After his stint with Herman, Shorty joined Charlie Barnet and then Stan Kenton, in whose band he played with and arranged for a young trumpet player from Canada named Maynard Ferguson. Then he settled in Los Angeles to apply himself to a dizzying variety of activities, from studio work to arranging to writing for films to leading his own group, Shorty Rogers and his Giants. In the latter capacity, he was considered a founding father of so-called West Coast jazz, which grew out of the resettlement in the Los Angeles area of a lot of gifted musicians after the golden days of the big bands had come to an end.

When it became fashionable for East Coast critics to denigrate the restrained and lyrical style of jazz that was being explored in California — reflecting a New York condescension toward California that still persists — Shorty Rogers was one of the targets. But some excellent music came out of that movement, if indeed it could be called a movement, and Shorty was one of its most artful practitioners, a supple, witty, and distinctive player whose solos could be identified in one or two bars, sometimes even in a single phrase. The command of form implicit in all his solos reflects his experience and abilities as a composer.

Slow-spoken and gentle in manner, Shorty is a warm and generous man. He was born two days before Henry Mancini, whom he met when they were traveling big band musicians. And thereby hangs a tale.

HENRY MANCINI

Born: Cleveland, Ohio, April 16, 1924

In 1958, RCA Victor Records expressed interest in the score of a new private-eye TV show, *Peter Gunn*. The music was by Henry Mancini, a composer then largely unknown to the public. It was the first all-jazz score for a TV series, utilizing some of the best musicians who had settled in California as the Big Band Era ended. The company approached Shorty Rogers, then a hot seller in the jazz field. Shorty urged Mancini to record the music himself. The company reluctantly allowed Mancini to make the album. It stayed on the sales charts more than two years and sold more than one million copies, unprecedented for a jazz album.

That album established Henry Mancini as a household name and opened a career for him in concerts and recordings that is without parallel in movie history. Although jazz had been used occasionally in small doses in movies and television, *Peter Gunn* set the precedent for other composers to use it extensively in film scores.

The son of Italian immigrants, Henry Mancini grew up in poverty in a small Pennsylvania steel town called West Aliquippa, and heard his first jazz from black musicians on the riverboats that passed by. He studied flute and arranging, briefly attended Juilliard, got drafted after Pearl Harbor, went overseas as a rifleman, then got into a military band which, he is convinced, saved his life. After the war he was pianist and arranger for the Tex Beneke band, successor to the Glenn Miller Orchestra. He had always dreamed of writing film scores, and Ginny O'Connor, a young singer with a vocal group that traveled with the band, urged him to settle in California and seek the career he wanted. He married her, and they set up housekeeping in the San Fernando Valley. Mancini got a job at Universal Pictures and learned his craft writing music for Abbott and Costello comedies, *Francis the Talking Mule*, and cheap horror pictures such as *Creature from the Black Lagoon*. When the young director Blake Edwards asked him to do the music for *Peter Gunn*, he was ready. There followed a succession of Edwards films, including *Breakfast at Tiffany's* and the *Pink Panther* series.

In November 1987, Hank asked me to accompany him to Pennsylvania. One morning we drove a rented car out to West Aliquippa, a community almost entirely deserted with the decline of the American steel industry. Hank found the house in which he had grown up. Its paint was peeling, and it was abandoned. He sat on the front step for a time absorbed in thought. Then we drove back to Pittsburgh. That night he conducted the Pittsburgh Symphony in a concert of his music.

Hank is drily self-deprecating. I once asked how tall he was. He said, "Six one," then grinned: "Six two when I've got a hit!"

JULIUS GUBENKO (TERRY GIBBS)

Born: Brooklyn, New York, October 13, 1924

The vibraphone is a peculiar instrument, modeled on the marimba and the xylophone. Its metal bars, laid out like the keyboard of the piano, are struck by mallets. It is not a sectional instrument, like trumpet, trombone, and saxophone. It is not even a necessary instrument in jazz. (The rhythm section instruments are; they help propel the music forward and lay its harmonic foundation.) Vibraphone can occasionally be used to add color to an orchestration, but that's about it. It has only one function in jazz: to play solos. If you choose this instrument, you have two choices. You either become a soloist of the front rank, or go into another line of work. In consequence, there have been fewer than a dozen important jazz vibraphonists, among them Adrian Rollini, Lionel Hampton, Red Norvo, Milt Jackson — and Terry Gibbs.

Terry's bright, confident, quick, energetic patterns of speech reflect his Brooklyn origins, and are reflected in turn in his playing. At twelve, he won a Major Bowes amateur contest on radio and toured with one of its units. After three years in the army, some of that time playing drums in a military band, he worked briefly with Tommy Dorsey. (A lot of people worked only briefly for the irascible Dorsey.) Then Terry toured Sweden with bassist Chubby Jackson, and in 1948 went with Woody Herman. It was with Herman — who liked the vibraphone, and had showcased Red Norvo and Margie Hyams on the instrument — that he came to prominence.

Since then, Terry has been one of the leading players of the instrument, noted for the energy and drive of his work. In the 1950s Terry formed a big band of California musicians. It was not, to be sure, a working road band — this was becoming increasingly impractical — but one whose personnel come together periodically to turn out some fiery music and make records. From time to time he has co-led a sextet with clarinetist Buddy DeFranco. Whatever the context, Terry is always in charge — and charging straight ahead.

ALBERT THORNTON (AL) GREY

Born: Aldie, Virginia, June 6, 1925

MICHAEL GREY

Born: Philadelphia, Pennsylvania, September 11, 1957

Jazz trombone has a strong tradition of humor. But then, humor inheres in the instrument, which is capable of all sorts of swoops and slides. When the plunger mute — the business end of a plumber's helper — is applied to the bell, an almost labial articulation results. Only a few men have mastered this technique. One of them is Al Grey (right in photograph), a gifted and serious trombonist on the one hand and a very funny one on the other.

Al's father was a trumpet player in Pottstown, Pennsylvania, where Al grew up and still lives. When Al was a boy, he took his father's horn out of the case, tried to play it, and bent a valve. His father beat him. Al's mother got a job scrubbing floors on her hands and knees in a music store to buy the boy a trombone. His father taught him to play it. Throughout his youth, Al was forbidden by his father to play baseball. Only later did Al realize why: he didn't want the boy to get hit in the mouth with a ball.

Al played through the bands of Benny Carter, Lucky Millinder, Lionel Hampton, Dizzy Gillespie, and Count Basie, then worked in all manner of small groups — proof of his adaptability. One of Al's four sons, Michael, turned out to have a gift for the trombone, too, and Al sent him to Boston's Berklee College of Music. A fellow student was Joe Cohn, son of Al's close friend, the late saxophonist Al Cohn. When Al Cohn was dying, Al Grey promised to keep an eye out for Joe, an excellent guitarist and trumpet player. And so he did: he formed a group whose members included Joe and Michael.

There is a technique called circular breathing that a very few saxophone and brass players have mastered: filling the cheeks with air and holding a note while inhaling through the nose. It makes possible long uninterrupted lines. Michael can do it. Al says affectionately, "If he thinks his old man is playing too much on him, he'll string me out by hitting on a note and holding it and holding it until the people applaud. Then he'll turn his head, 'You see, Dad?'"

OSCAR EMMANUEL PETERSON

Born: Montreal, Quebec, August 15, 1925

Hank Jones has said, "Oscar Peterson is head and shoulders above any pianist alive today. Oscar is at the apex. He is the crowning ruler of all the pianists in the jazz world. No question about it." André Previn says emphatically, "He is the *best.*" When I surveyed seventy pianists on the subject of jazz piano, the close winners in the categories of personal favorite and "best" pianist were Art Tatum, Bill Evans, and Oscar Peterson. Oscar was Bill's favorite pianist. He is Roger Kellaway's favorite pianist. Dizzy Gillespie cites him as one of his favorite pianists to play *with*. Critic Leonard Feather said that if he were to be reincarnated, he would want to come back as Oscar Peterson.

Peterson is the son of a Montreal railway porter and former ship's bos'n who taught music to his five children. One of them was his daughter Daisy, who then became Oscar's teacher. Oscar went on to study with Paul de Marky, a Hungarian pianist who had studied in Budapest with Istvan Toman, whose teacher in turn was Franz Liszt. Oscar was already well known in Canada when he burst on the rest of the world in 1949 during a Jazz at the Philharmonic concert at Carnegie Hall. Since then, he has been at the pinnacle of jazz piano, a virtuoso whose playing has roots in the bravura of Liszt.

Oscar has led trios since the early 1950s, played solo recitals all over the world, explored the world of electronic music, and worked extensively with young people. Now he dedicates himself more and more to composition. Oscar suffered the slings and snubs of outrageous racism in Montreal in his youth. This has led him to take a staunch public stand against racism in Canada and elsewhere. In 1973 he was invested as a Companion of the Order of Canada, and afterwards told me almost shyly, "I never thought my country would honor me this way." It continues to do so. In 1991 he was appointed Chancellor of York University in Toronto and received a Toronto Arts Award for lifetime musical achievment. At my last count he had ten honorary doctorates in music.

JOHN ALFRED (JOHNNY) MANDEL

Born: New York City, November 23, 1925

The ability to write melody is mysterious. There are trained arrangers and composers who lack it, and untrained musicians who have it. Two of the latter were Frank Loesser and Irving Berlin. There are even a few trained musicians who have it, including Tchaikovsky, Henry Mancini—and Johnny Mandel.

Johnny was a child prodigy on brass instruments. He attended New York Military Academy, studied arranging with Van Alexander, and during the Second World War, joined the band of Henry Jerome, in which a lot of important jazz musicians got their first experience. Some other types, too. "While I was in it, Leonard Garment and Alan Greenspan were in the sax section," Mandel recalls. "Lenny Garment was studying law and Alan Greenspan was taking economics. When Alan Greenspan left, Al Cohn took his place." Later Leonard Garment became a powerful figure in the Republican Party, while Greenspan became chairman of the Federal Reserve Board.

Johnny switched from trumpet to trombone, and joined the Boyd Raeburn band, then Jimmy Dorsey's, and Buddy Rich's bands, and then Alvino Ray. He took time off to study at the Manhattan School of Music. He wrote for Latin bands, contributed to the book of the 1949 Artie Shaw orchestra, and composed for television. In time, Johnny gave up playing and settled in Los Angeles where he began to freelance, writing arrangements for albums by the likes of Frank Sinatra. He broke into film scoring, where he at last had the chance to indulge his love of melody.

He composed the exquisite "Emily" for the 1964 film *The Americanization of Emily*, and "The Shadow of Your Smile" for the 1965 picture *The Sandpiper*. For the latter film, he scored the scenery—the magnificent mountains and surf of California's Big Sur country.

He continues to write arrangements for jazz players and singers, including charts for the 1991 hit vocal album by Natalie Cole, *Unforgettable*, for which he received a Grammy award.

CLIFFORD (BUD) SHANK

Born: Dayton, Ohio, May 27, 1926

No one illustrates the way jazz expresses the inner states of its practitioners better than Bud Shank. Bud was part of that lyrical approach to the music disparaged by New York critics and some musicians as West Coast jazz. Bud's playing on saxophones, chiefly alto, and on flute, had a deferential quality that lacked the testosterone level certain easterners seemed to think was a defining quality of jazz.

Bud, an alumnus of the Stan Kenton band, was a stalwart of the Los Angeles recording scene. You often heard his lovely sound in movie scores. "I was a studio sausage," he puts it. He found solace in driving Formula One racing cars and sailing his boats, meanwhile putting his gains into California real estate back when its prices were not yet challenging those of downtown Tokyo.

Then, abruptly, Bud left the studios, and even left California, taking residence in Port Townsend, Washington, where he founded a summertime festival of the arts and a teaching program for young jazz musicians. So handsome in his youth that one might almost have described him as pretty, he grew a gray beard and took on the look of a mountain man. He gave up the flute, arguing that no one can master two instruments, and devoted himself to playing jazz on the alto.

His playing changed radically. I was mystified. Then Bud and I had a long talk and I learned why. Bud was cross-eyed from childhood. I told him I had never noticed. He said, "No, you didn't. I had ways to conceal it." Turning his head away from you. Wearing sunglasses. All sorts of tricks. "And," he said, "I played like that too."

A doctor told him he could fix that eye. He could not restore its sight, of course. (A wayward eye eventually loses its sight; the brain refuses to process the signal from it.) Bud thought it over and submitted to the surgery. The eye is now straight. Bud is no longer ashamed. He holds his head up, looks right at you, and plays that way. His playing has become fiery, proud, defiant.

GENEVIEVE HERING (JERI SOUTHERN)

Born: Royal, Nebraska, August 5, 1926

Someone called Jeri Southern the Greta Garbo of jazz. Like Garbo and Artie Shaw —and like Rossini, Sibelius, Charles Ives, Umberto Giordano, and a few more—Jeri walked away from a career at its peak.

She was trained as a pianist and as an opera singer. Jeri told me (and at first I thought she was wrong) that each of us has two voices, a speaking voice and a singing voice. She demonstrated by tossing off a couple of operatic measures in a huge voice I didn't realize she had. It was, she said, when she started to sing in her speaking voice that her career took off. She turned out a series of recordings that established her as a star. The best known was probably "You'd Better Go Now."

But Jeri was terrified of performing, while at the same time bored by it. She hated seeing her name on a nightclub marquee, hated the pressure of expectation in an audience's eyes, hated standing there in a spotlight in an expensive and, in her view, phony gown. Her philosophy of performing was the exact opposite of Carmen McRae's. Once Jeri got a song the way she wanted it, she kept it that way and then grew bored by it.

So she simply quit. Even twenty years later she was beging offered huge sums to do just a single evening's performance. She refused. She spent the rest of her life teaching piano and voice.

Jeri was at one time married to composer and arranger Bill Holman. They remained friends long after their divorce. She had a long love affair with one of my closest friends, the late film composer Hugo Friedhofer, more than twenty-five years her senior, and orchestrated his last score, a documentary on forest life. She was a remarkable musician and a superbly lyrical pianist.

Jeri was working on the piano arrangements for the songs of one of her good friends, Peggy Lee, whom I happened to phone one sunny afternoon in the late summer of 1991.

"How're you doing?" I asked.

"I'm very sad," Peggy said. "Jeri Southern died this morning." The date was August 4, 1991.

ANTHONY BENEDETTO (TONY BENNETT)

Born: New York City, August 23, 1926

Jazz has always drawn on popular music for material, while at the same time influencing it. George Gershwin, Harold Arlen, and many other composers for Broadway and Tin Pan Alley have reflected that influence, along with many of the singers of their songs, among them Lee Wiley and Frank Sinatra. None has been more deeply affected by jazz than Tony Bennett, whose reverence for Louis Armstrong is manifest even in his vibrato.

Tony doesn't consider himself a jazz artist. Many of the jazz musicians who have worked with him would disagree, and the way he phrases, the way he feels time, the passion, the intensity of his work all reflect his love of jazz and commitment to the music. And in the late eighties, CBS Records issued a two-disc album titled *Tony Bennett Jazz*, a retrospective of his work with Ralph Burns, Herbie Hancock, Stan Getz, and others.

Tony considers that his finishing school was the Count Basie band, with which he toured. He always works with jazz musicians, and he recorded two exceptional albums with the late Bill Evans.

The creative passion often manifests itself in more than one art, and a number of jazz musicians—Miles Davis, Mel Powell, George Wettling, John Heard—have been capable and, in some cases, excellent painters. Tony's oils sell for large sums.

Tony tends to think of himself as a New York street kid, and despite the success he had with his recording of "I Left My Heart in San Francisco," New Yorkers often think of him as one of their own. Tony speaks with the greatest pleasure about the day he was walking down a New York street and a worker stuck his head out of a manhole and called, "Hi, Tony!" But fame has another side. Once, a long time ago, when I was talking to him on the telephone, I said, "Hey, why don't we get your kids and go out to the World's Fair this afternoon?" Tony reminded me that he couldn't walk down its midway without getting mobbed.

Tony has a particular significance in my life. He was the first major singer to record my songs, and he has recorded more of them than any other. One is "Yesterday I Heard the Rain," a lyric I wrote at his request. I once tried to thank him for this. I told him, "You and Woody Herman discovered me."

Tony replied instantly, "No! That's wrong. *You* discovered you."

GERALD JOSEPH (GERRY) MULLIGAN

Born: New York City, April 6, 1927

Ah yes. The Irishman. What shall I say of Gerald Joseph? When I became editor of *Down Beat* early in 1959, I consulted two or three of my predecessors in that chair. I asked Jack Tracy which of the musicians I would have trouble with. He said without hesitation, "Miles Davis, Buddy Rich, and Gerry Mulligan." Perhaps because I was thus forewarned, I had no trouble with any of them; Gerry became a close friend and so remains. I think the world of Gerry. And that's entirely aside from my respect for him as a musician: premier soloist on the baritone and soprano saxophones, pianist, composer, orchestrator, and all-round major innovator. His participation, as composer and player, in the early Miles Davis *Birth of the Cool* album (a misnomer, but one that persists) served to spread his influence around the world. Antonio Carlos Jobim and other Brazilian composers told me that Gerry was a big influence on them. He was considered the central figure of so-called West Coast jazz, though he was a native of New York, grew up in Reading, Pennsylvania, and evolved as a young musician in Philadelphia.

Gerry's first arrangements were recorded when he was only eighteen. He wrote for drummer and bandleader Gene Krupa and for the enormously influential Claude Thornhill band, where he came under the influence of Gil Evans. Then he founded a piano-less quartet with the late Chet Baker on trumpet. A series of quartets followed, then a big band. Witty, funny, proud, restless, searching, eternally curious about music and life and books and linguistics and history and just about anything you could name, Gerry lives in two places, Darien, Connecticut, and Milan, Italy, with his Italian wife Franca, a journalist he met when she covered one of his record dates.

Gerry was a young man when I met him, one of the Young Turks. Now he is one of the elder statesmen, and it startles me to see him with that red-blond hair long since gone white and that white beard. I always told him he had the map of Erin plastered on his kisser. Now he looks like a tall Irish elf. Play on, old friend.

WILLIS LEONARD (BILL) HOLMAN

Born: Olive, California, May 21, 1927

With the rise of the big bands in the 1920s and thirties, a new kind of musician came to prominence: the arranger. One of the pioneers in this field was Bill Challis. Unlike in the classical music field, arrangers for big bands — jazz or otherwise — usually arranged the music of other composers, songs drawn from the pop catalogue. In the work of the best of them, people like Don Redman, Fletcher Henderson, Benny Carter, Sy Oliver, Pete Rugolo, Gil Evans, Ralph Burns, and Johnny Mandel, the act of arranging amounted to re-composition. And some of these people went further, writing new pieces which, in the peculiarly unpretentious language of jazz, were seldom if ever referred to as compositions. Turning an adjective into a noun, musicians called them "originals."

Bill Holman is one of the most respected of these composers and arrangers. In 1966, he put aside his saxophone to devote himself entirely to writing. Bill's work contributed immeasurably to the book (as a band's collection of arrangements is called) of Stan Kenton, with whose name Holman became strongly associated. But Holman wrote for many other bands, including those of Gerry Mulligan, Woody Herman, and Buddy Rich. At one point he was co-leader of a quintet with the late Mel Lewis, who was himself a seminal influence in jazz.

Bill is one of those arrangers who shows sympathy and sensitivity toward singers; he wrote some excellent charts (as jazz musicians call arrangements; occasionally they're called "maps") for Sarah Vaughan, Peggy Lee, and most recently Natalie Cole.

From time to time Holman leads a big band of his own in the Los Angeles area, and it is in this context that his swinging, fresh, impeccably tasteful writing is heard at its best. Not all gifted arrangers are also good composers. Bill Holman assuredly is both.

ROMANO MUSSOLINI

Born: Carpena (Forli), Italy, September 26, 1927

Twentieth-century dictatorships of both the left and right have been consistently hostile to jazz. Even in the darkest night of Nazism, however, young Germans were guarding their jazz records jealously.

And in Rome, the third son of Benito Mussolini was listening to the jazz collection of his brothers Bruno and Vittorio. After the brutal execution of his father in 1945—and the death of most of his family — Romano Mussolini, along with his mother and sister, fled mainland Italy to Ischia, a volcanic island at the west entrance of the Bay of Naples. There he fell seriously ill. While recovering, he began to teach himself accordion and piano, both instruments played by George Shearing, on whom he modeled his playing. He returned to Rome and lived in poverty. When he began playing professionally he used the name Romano Full, but word of his identity got around; he could hardly escape it. Gradually he overcame it. He played at the first Festivale Internazionale del Jazz in San Remo in 1956. In 1959, he toured with Lars Gullin, Chet Baker, and singer Caterina Valente.

Ironically, he is best known in America for a story about Chet Baker, so improbable that I thought for years that it was apocryphal. Then Caterina Valente assured me of its truth. "I was there!" she said.

Chet Baker was the archetype of the spaced-out jazz musician of bebop jokes, a myth that had only a few counterparts in reality. But he was for real. When he was introduced to Romano Mussolini at the start of that 1959 tour, the two shook hands and Chet said, "Sorry to hear about your old man."

Romano Mussolini survived even that. He is accepted by musicians for his work, for a warm and open temperament, and for his dry sense of humor. He is a well-liked man, and a fixture of the Roman jazz world. In recent years he has been making appearances in the United States and Canada. One of the American musicians with whom he has recorded is Spiegle Willcox.

He is married to a sister of Sophia Loren.

ROBERT RODNEY CHUDNICK (RED RODNEY)

Born: Philadelphia, Pennsylvania, September 27, 1927

When Red Rodney was ten, his father gave him a bugle and enrolled him in a drum and bugle corps at a Jewish war veterans' post. He got his first trumpet three years later. During the Second World War, when musicians were being drafted, he played as a substitute in various big bands that came to Atlantic City. For a time he worked in a CBS radio orchestra led by Elliott Lawrence. One of the arrangers for that band was a young man only a little older than he was, Gerry Mulligan.

Red played in the Claude Thornhill orchestra when Gil Evans and Gerry were on its arranging staff, and then with the Woody Herman band in its Four Brothers period. One of his mates in the trumpet section was Shorty Rogers, who was also one of the band's chief arrangers. Shorty would assign trumpet solos not to himself but to Red.

Red aspired to bebop and left the Herman band to hang around New York with his friends and fellow trumpeters Miles Davis, Fats Navarro, and Kenny Dorham. Then in late 1949 he joined a group led by his idol and mentor, Charlie Parker. He stayed three years.

Far from extolling heroin, Parker tried to keep Red away from the drug, using himself as the horrible example of its ravages. It was futile. "When I listened to that genius night after night," Red said, "being young and immature and not an educated person, I must have thought, 'If I crossed over that line, could I play like that?' " When Parker found out that Red had become addicted, he was furious.

Red is an ardent and eloquent spokesperson against drugs. His habit landed him several times in prisons and rehabilitation centers. In time he kicked his habit and gained control of his life, which suddenly seemed very sunny. A group he formed with trumpeter and saxophonist Ira Sullivan brought both of them back to public attention. Then he set up a group of his own, and as he entered his sixties was playing more brilliantly than ever, now one of the old masters and one of the great mentors of the young.

He likes to quote Art Blakey on the subject of jazz: "If you pass through this life without hearing this music, you've missed a great deal."

ERNEST MITCHELL (ERNIE) ANDREWS

Born: Philadelphia, Pennsylvania, December 25, 1927

Stories of injustice abound in the music business, case after case of gifted people never receiving the recognition they deserve — or being cheated of money when they are recognized. One of the most flagrant cases is that of Ernie Andrews. The blues singer Jimmy Witherspoon thinks Ernie is the best singer in the business, and Witherspoon assuredly is one of the best himself. A similar high opinion is held by pianist and arranger Nat Pierce and drummer Frank Capp, with whose Juggernaut band Ernie often appears. Yet you can search through jazz encyclopedias and dictionaries in vain for mention of Ernie, and one of the few that does take note of his existence dismisses him in six lines. He deserves much more. Ernie is a vital and very individual performer, as much at home in the blues as in ballads.

Music was in the family. "My mother," Ernie says, "was a great singer, a Baptist singer. So was my father. He was from Virginia, my mother from Louisiana." Ernie left Philadelphia for New Orleans when he was twelve or thirteen to play drums and study under Bunk Johnson. He moved to California at the age of fifteen and made his first vocal records of sixteen for songwriter and producer Joe Green. He recorded, at his own best count, for nineteen labels over the years, including Decca and Columbia. "I made my debut in New York in 1954 with Jimmy Jones on piano, Earl May on bass, and Percy Bryce on drums, at Birdland. Opposite Dizzy Gillespie and Charlie Parker! I was scared to death! Charlie Parker used to come up to me every night and sing 'When you open it to speak,' because he wanted me to do 'My Funny Valentine' every night."

Ernie joined the Harry James band in 1959 and stayed for ten years. "I had a wonderful time with Buddy Rich and Sonny Payne and all the great musicians who played in that band," he says. "And Harry was like my father. He was lovely person, man. He gave me so much knowledge of this business. He was a sweetheart. It was great."

Ernie has recorded with Jay McShann, Benny Carter, Clark Terry, Sahib Shihab, Mel Lewis, Al Grey, and Ernie Wilkins. He went on the road in 1959 with Ray Brown, and in 1989 he toured extensively with pianist Gene Harris.

Ernie's latest album appearance, *You Can Hide Inside the Music,* is a particular favorite. He recorded with two of the best of today's younger musicians, the Harper brothers, who augmented their sextet with the addition of trumpeter Harry (Sweets) Edison and organist Jimmy McGriff.

"I am glad we could record with some of our heroes," trumpeter Philip Harper said.

WILLIAM ORVAL (BILL) CROW

Born: Othello, Washington, December 27, 1927

As mentioned in the Foreword, one is always reading somewhere that "jazz musicians are not usually articulate men." They are in fact very verbal, often highly educated in several fields, and usually literate. A psychologist with an interest in jazz once put it this way: "They have used their road time well" — meaning, they have used those long hours in hotel rooms to read voraciously. A number of them have even become able writers, among them cornetist Rex Stewart, who wrote a book on jazz, drummer Dave Tough, who wrote a column for *Down Beat*, and pianist Don Asher, who, like Artie Shaw, is author of a number of books. A prime example of the jazzman-who-writes is Bill Crow.

Bill is a versatile musician who first worked as a drummer and trombonist. Two years after he took up the bass, he joined Stan Getz. Subsequently he played with Terry Gibbs, Marian McPartland, Al Cohn and Zoot Sims, the Bob Brookmeyer-Clark Terry quintet, and Benny Goodman, with whom he made the famous 1962 tour of the Soviet Union. His best-known association has been with Gerry Mulligan. He worked in the Mulligan quartet with Art Farmer, and later with the late Mel Lewis constituted the rhythm section of the Gerry Mulligan Concert Band.

Bill started writing perceptive jazz reviews back in the 1960s. His abilities as a writer continued to grow to the point where he now has in effect, a second career as an author. In 1990, Oxford University Press published his book *Jazz Anec-*

dotes, in which Bill recounted some of the funniest stories jazz musicians tell about each other. He was soon at work on a second book, *From Birdland to Broadway*, published in the fall of 1992. All the while Bill remains active as one of the really fine bassists in jazz and as a member of the musicians' union in New York.

MORRIS (MOE) KOFFMAN

Born: Toronto, Ontario, January 20, 1928

In 1958, Moe Koffman managed to make an international hit record with a jazz composition and performance, his "Swinging Shepherd Blues." The record did a great deal to establish the flute as a legitimate jazz instrument. However, since a certain element among jazz admirers like to think of the art as arcane and therefore are suspicious of success, the record actually served to diminish Moe's reputation and obscure his very real abilities as a jazz saxophonist and flutist.

Like most jazz musicians, Koffman obtained a thorough academic foundation in music. He had excellent teachers at the Toronto Conservatory of Music, and in New York he studied flute with Harold Bennett of the Metropolitan Opera orchestra and clarinet with Leon Russianoff of the New York Philharmonic. Meanwhile he worked in the big bands of Sonny Dunham and Jimmy Dorsey.

Later, in Toronto, he was active in a bewildering variety of musical circumstances, leading a quartet or a quintet of his own that often included the fine guitarist Ed Bickert. Moe recorded in all manner of contexts, from jazz groups to television orchestras to advertising jingles. He made a few "jazz classics" albums, including *Master Sessions*, some of which reflected his love of Bach. Whatever the context, the quality of his playing was never compromised. He has made perhaps thirty albums.

Moe was a devotee of bebop from his earliest days, and its aesthetic still permeates his playing. In recent years he has toured a good deal and recorded with the great bebop trumpeter who was one of his early idols, John Birks Gillespie. But perhaps his most important exposure as the serious player he is has been in the Rob McConnell Boss Brass. His solos and section work on soprano and alto saxophones and on flute left no doubt with any serious listener to that orchestra that Moe Koffman is one superb jazz musician. And, incidentally, one of Dizzy Gillespie's favorites.

HAROLD DE VANCE LAND

Born: Houston, Texas, February 18, 1928

The terminology of jazz has often been misleading, no expression more so than "West Coast jazz." This was used to indicate a soft, lyrical school of playing as represented by Gerry Mulligan, Bud Shank, Shorty Rogers, and Chet Baker. But most of its prominent players were from the East. And the West Coast natives in turn were often some of the finest practitioners of what became known as hard bop, a school usually associated with New York.

One of the "hard" players is Harold Land who, though born in Texas, grew up in San Diego. He became interested in music in high school and started playing tenor saxophone when he was sixteen years old, which is comparatively late. After moving to Los Angeles he replaced Teddy Edwards in the Max Roach Quintet. The trumpeter with the group at that time was Clifford Brown. Harold stayed with Max for eighteen months, then worked with bassist Curtis Counce. He led his own groups, and co-led groups with bassist Red Mitchell, vibraphonist Bobby Hutcherson, and trumpeter Blue Mitchell. In the 1950s he was a member of the big band led by composer Gerald Wilson. Once he worked as a sideman with Thelonious Monk. Harold has recorded with his own groups. One of his best-known albums is *The Fox*, made in 1959 with Elmo Hope, Dupree Bolton, Herbie Lewis, and Frank Butler. He has also recorded with trumpeters Kenny Dorham and Carmell Jones, and guitarist Wes Montgomery.

Harold presents another example of the tendency of music to run in families. His son, Harold Land Jr., is a pianist and composer who has worked with Kenny Burrell, Gerald Wilson, and of course his father.

Harold Sr. continues to work as a freelance in Los Angeles. His playing is daring, very individual, and strong, and it is widely held among musicians that Harold has never received the recognition he deserves. I concur in that judgment. He is a simply beautiful player.

LOUIS A. (LOU) LEVY

Born: Chicago, Illinois, March 5, 1928

Lou Levy is two things that seem incompatible: the archetype of the bebop pianist and the most sympathetic possible accompanist for singers, including three of the best: Sarah Vaughan, Ella Fitzgerald, and Peggy Lee. Peggy calls him "my good gray fox," both for the color of his hair and the clever yet sympathetic nature of his accompaniment.

He began studying piano when he was nine or ten, and in the fervent early days of bebop, he listened in fascination to the records of Charlie Parker and Dizzy Gillespie. At the same time, he was taking in two major piano influences, Bud Powell and Art Tatum. He began to work professionally in 1947 with the band of saxophonist Georgie Auld. That same year he accompanied Sarah Vaughan, then joined the band of Chubby Jackson. In 1948, Lou went with the great Woody Herman Second Herd, the bop band that featured saxophonists Zoot Sims, Al Cohn, and Stan Getz.

In 1950 he joined Tommy Dorsey, who fired him with the words: "Kid, you play good. But not for my band."

"And he was right," Lou says. "I didn't like it and he didn't like it."

He never got fired again.

Lou settled in California, where he became a staple of the studios, recording with Conte Candoli, Shorty Rogers, and Stan Getz, among other Herman alumni. Once again, he worked with singers: June Christy, Anita O'Day, Lena Horne, Nancy Wilson, Tony Bennett, and Frank Sinatra. He played with Stan Getz, Terry Gibbs,

Benny Goodman, and the group known as Supersax, which specialized in the solos of Charlie Parker orchestrated for five saxophones.

Of those jazz pianists who are reluctant to accompany singers, Lou says simply, "They're crazy." He has a love for the words of songs. It is manifest in the way he plays. He has had a long personal relationship with Pinky Winters, a subtle and sensitive singer little heard outside California, and together they teach a course on the art of accompaniment.

For all of his modesty — and it is real, not affected — Lou, in an instrumental setting, is a fleet, inventive, brilliant soloist.

MAYNARD FERGUSON

Born: Verdun, Quebec, May 4, 1928

Maynard Ferguson was born in the Montreal suburb of Verdun, only blocks from Oscar Peterson's birthplace. Maynard's and Oscar's lives converged when they attended Montreal High School and played in a band led by Maynard's brother, Percy.

One of Maynard's assignments at Montreal High was to play trumpet during the morning flag-raising, even in winter. Maynard would stand there in the bitter cold playing his horn while Oscar watched from the warmth of the building, laughing maniacally.

Maynard used to practice along with the records of Harry James, famous, among other things, for his high notes. Maynard would equal them and then go higher. Soon, leading his own band, he was astounding visiting musicians with his unprecedented upper register — not just squeals and squeaks, but controlled tones up to a double high C.

He played in the big bands of Boyd Raeburn and Charlie Barnet in the late 1940s. One musician who heard him was Pete Rugolo, then with Stan Kenton's band. Kenton hired Maynard in 1950. Shorty Rogers, who was in the trumpet section of the band and wrote pieces for Kenton that featured Maynard, said, "I couldn't believe I was writing notes that high for the trumpet."

Maynard formed his own thirteen-piece Dream Band, and has led his own groups — from combos to a sixteen-piece group made up entirely of British musicians — since the mid-1950s.

He has lived in England and India (where he went to meditate) and the United States. We used to see each other in nightclubs and at festivals. Now he lives just down the street from me in the little mountain town of Ojai, California, and I run into him and his wife Flo at the supermarket.

Maynard plays all the brass instruments. He has been known to play trumpet, valve trombone, French horn, and euphonium during a single performance. As for his high register on trumpet, he equates it with the once unattainable four-minute mile and says with a laugh, "Now I've got two or three kids in my band who can play that high."

ARTHUR STEWART (ART) FARMER

Born: Council Bluffs, Iowa, August 21, 1928

Art and his twin brother Addison, of African and Blackfoot Indian antecedents, were taken at the age of four to Phoenix, Arizona, by their mother, after her divorce from their father. There were doctors and lawyers among his relatives, and Art and Addison spent those early years in the parsonage of the African Methodist Church, in which their grandfather was a minister. A cousin of John Lewis was one of Art's first music teachers. Art leaned to the brass instruments, Addison to the string bass. They looked so much alike that I once joked with Art, "How do you tell yourselves apart?" Without hesitation or a trace of a smile, Art replied, "When I wake up in the morning I pick up the bass. If I can't play it, I must be Art."

There was little for them to do in Phoenix and at the age of seventeen Art and Addison talked their mother into letting them move to Los Angeles. There they attended Jefferson High School, important in jazz history because it employed Samuel Browne who led the stage band and trained its young players. Saxophone greats Dexter Gordon and Frank Morgan both attended Jefferson High.

Eventually Art made his way to New York where he worked with various bands, including that of Lionel Hampton. He emerged as a highly lyrical soloist on both trumpet and fluegelhorn. In time he formed a group called the Jazztet with Benny Golson, but much of his career has been spent as a major soloist. Art lives in Vienna now.

Addison died in 1963 of a brain aneu-

rism. Art took him home to Phoenix for burial. Long afterwards Art told me, "Addison is still alive to me. I still have dreams about him. In the dreams we're doing this, doing that, talking, arguing, going some place, playing, practicing, rehearsing, traveling. The little things of life."

HORACE TAVARES SILVA (HORACE SILVER)

Born: Norwalk, Connecticut, September 2, 1928

If I have found one universal in the life of jazz musicians, it is parental support. I can think of no exception: there is always at least one parent who encouraged the love and study of music. This is particularly so in the case of Horace Silver, who is of mixed African, Portuguese, and American Indian ancestry.

His father was born in the Cape Verde Islands, which lie three hundred miles off the coast of Senegal, and emigrated with his brothers to New England. The Cape Verde Islands were a staging area for the exportation to the Americas of African slaves, and the population there became a mix of African and Portuguese. Thus Horace's very origins reflect the history of inhuman exploitation that eventually led to the birth of jazz itself. And his music reflects this ancestry: rich with influences of the blues, gospel music, the Cape Verdean folk music with which he was surrounded as a child, and the Jimmie Lunceford band his father took him to see at an open-air pavilion in an oceanside park near their home. The band was black, but blacks were not allowed to enter the pavilion: Horace and his father listened from outside, peering in through the slats in the pavilion wall. In 1964, Horace recorded the album *Song for My Father*. A number of his tunes echo his family history, including "Señor Blues" and "The Cape Verdean Blues."

Horace had good solid academic training and wishes he'd had even more. He developed into one of the major modern jazz musicians, not just as a pianist but as a writer. Almost all his recorded work with his various quintets has been of his own compositions, many of which have passed into the permanent jazz repertoire. Like Art Blakey, with whose Jazz Messengers he worked in his early career, he has been a major developer of other musicians, among them Donald Byrd, Hank Mobley, Art Farmer, the Brecker brothers, Stanley Clarke, Blue Mitchell, Bob Berg, Billy Cobham, Junior Cook, Roger Humphries, Roy Brooks, Louis Hayes, Tom Harrell, Joe Henderson, Carmen Jones, Clifford Jordan, Benny Maupin, Larry Ridley, Stanley Turrentine, Brian Lynch, and Ralph Moore.

Horace lives in Malibu, California, touring part of each year, still finding and developing young talent, and recording for his own Silveto label. He has a gentle quality about him and a sweet humility. Of the constant performances of his compositions by other groups, he says, "I am always honored that people remember my music and still want to record it." Remember it indeed. Such tunes as "Strollin'" and "Señor Blues" are unforgettable, a major part of the literature of modern jazz.

ALBERT MANGELSDORFF

Born: Frankfurt am Main, Germany, September 5, 1928

Though it entails the same sort of abilities that go into classical music—instrumental virtuosity and the skills of the composer—jazz differs from classical in an essential way. In the classical tradition, the composer is a monarch dictating to instrumentalists who strive to interpret his wishes. In jazz, the instrumentalist *is* a composer, albeit of spontaneous music (as opposed to what Bill Evans called "contemplative" music).

It is not surprising, then, that dictators have loathed it. While failing to understand it as a musical art form, they correctly perceived it as a challenge to authority. Hitler's minions denounced it as "Negroid-Jewish" music, and sent some of its players to death in concentration camps. This is the source of Dizzy Gillespie's comment, "Men have died for this music. You can't get more serious than that."

Even in Hitler's Germany the prohibition failed, for many gifted young Germans were enamored of jazz. One of these was Albert Mangelsdorff, who played violin and guitar before he took up trombone at the age of twenty. Albert played his way up through the different schools of jazz, through bebop into the contemporary free-jazz movement. He has played trombone in big bands and small groups, led quartets and quintets, and recorded in an enormous range of contexts, even solo. Yes, solo. He has developed a technique of bringing out the overtones on the trombone so that he can play actual chords on the instrument, called "multiphonics" by

some writers. Hearing him play in Chicago where he went to photograph Albert, John Reeves described the effect as resembling the sound of wind blowing across a thousand open beer bottles. It is quite startling. John Lewis, who in the early sixties recorded an album with Mangelsdorff titled *Animal Dances*, has called Albert "one of the three most important trombone players in jazz."

Gentle of manner, with the face of a German lyric poet, Mangelsdorff is one of those musicians who helped establish jazz as an international art form.

BENNY GOLSON

Born: Philadelphia, Pennsylvania, January 25, 1929

Often one finds that the friendships of prominent jazz musicians go back to seminal high schools such as Cass Tech in Detroit, Wendell Phillips and Austin high schools in Chicago, Granoff in Philadelphia, and Jefferson High in Los Angeles. And even when they do not originate in the same school, many such relationships go back to early youth. One such case is that of Benny Golson and a boy from North Carolina named John Coltrane. They grew up together musically, playing in rowdy local commercial bands to learn their craft. And they got fired together from one. Benny's mother consoled them: "One day both of you are going to be so good that that band will not be able to afford you."

Benny studied music at Howard University, whose faculty officially frowned on jazz. The saxophone was not considered an "appropriate" instrument. Benny signed up for clarinet and practiced the saxophone in the laundry room, where no one could hear him. Already, composition was one of his main interests. He grew impatient with the academic rigidity he found at Howard and left before graduation, joining the band of Bull Moose Jackson and going on the road. He worked with Tadd Dameron and the big bands of Lionel Hampton (1953) and Dizzy Gillespie (1956-57), then joined drummer Art Blakey, with whom he worked in 1958 and '59. Blakey, like Horace Silver, was a major mentor of young jazzmen, and Benny's reputation, both as a composer and player, grew. Many of Golson's compositions, such as "Killer Joe" and "I Remember Clifford," have become part of the permanent jazz repertoire. In 1959, he and Art Farmer —a Silver and Gerry Mulligan alumnus— formed their Jazztet, a sextet that at first featured trombonist Curtis Fuller and Art's brother Addison on bass. The group lasted until 1962.

Then Benny broke into television and film scoring in Hollywood, writing scores at all the major studios. He moved back to New York City in 1987, where he soon found himself busier than he had ever been, in all forms of composition and as a player too. In May 1992, Benny was awarded an honorary doctorate by William Paterson College. He teaches there.

One year, backstage at the Newport Jazz Festival, Benny ran into John Coltrane, who reminded him of the time they got fired in Philadelphia. "Remember what your mother said?" John asked. "Do you think they'd be able to afford us now?"

ANDREAS LUDWIG PREWIN (ANDRÉ PREVIN)

Born: Berlin, Germany, April 6, 1929

A jazz-loving judge from Jamaica once remarked that jazz was America's gift to the world. André Previn is the gift of jazz to the symphony orchestra. The division between jazz and classical music has always been more apparent than real, and from its earliest days major classical composers and conductors have admired and championed jazz. But André is the first jazz musician to become one of the world's major symphony conductors.

André's father was a lawyer and judge of Russian Jewish descent. As a child he studied piano at the Berlin Hochschule für Musik. The family left Berlin in 1938 as Hitler's persecution of the Jews grew more virulent. They lived for a year in France, where André studied piano and theory at the Paris Conservatory. Then they fled to America, settling in Los Angeles, where an important community of artistic émigrés, including Arnold Schoenberg, Thomas Mann, Igor Stravinsky, Ernst Toch, Bertolt Brecht, Christopher Isherwood, and Aldous Huxley had taken residence.

André was an arranger at MGM when he was still in high school. Fascinated — like so many other pianists — by Art Tatum, André made jazz recordings when he was only sixteen, revealing an almost stupefying technical command. He was simply an amazing pianist, regardless of idiom.

André has been successful in every field of music he has touched: as a jazz pianist (an album of compositions from *My Fair Lady*, recorded in the mid-fifties with drummer Shelly Manne and bassist Leroy Vinnegar, remains popular), as a composer for films and Broadway, as a music director in motion pictures, as an orchestrator, and, after he grew bored by it all and disgusted with show biz, as a symphony conductor. He has been the music director of the Houston Symphony, the London Symphony, the Pittsburgh Symphony, the Los Angeles Philharmonic, and the Royal Philharmonic. He is a regular guest conductor of the Vienna Philharmonic, the Dresden Staatskapelle, the Concertgebouw Orchestra, and the Berlin Philharmonic. His orchestral recordings of Ralph Vaughan Williams and Rachmaninoff, among others, are considered major and perhaps definitive. Composer Mel Powell says that in the contemporary classical music world, André is widely considered the best conductor alive. Composer David Raksin says that "in some unfortunate way, he is taken for granted. He makes everything look too easy, so much so that people who can't even pick up a baton think they can conduct. It's what I call an inadvertent populism."

André is a funny raconteur whose stories may come to you in French or German, which he still speaks as comfortably as he does English.

He continues to record jazz, often with Ray Brown and Mundell Lowe.

ROBERT (BOB) BROOKMEYER

Born: Kansas City, Kansas, December 19, 1929

Brooks, as many of his friends call him, is sometimes identified with the West Coast school of jazz, in part because he replaced Chet Baker (in 1953) in the Gerry Mulligan Quartet. Generally, though, Bob has managed to escape categorization, perhaps because his principal instrument is one that only a few musicians have used in jazz, the valve trombone. Bob studied at the Kansas City Conservatory and originally played piano; he took up the valve trombone when he was twenty-three, and almost immediately became a major figure in jazz.

Most of Bob's career has been in New York, working with almost every major jazzman there, but most significantly Clark Terry, with whom he co-led a quintet. His association with Mulligan continued, and when Mulligan formed his concert band, Brookmeyer played in it along with Zoot Sims, Bill Crow, Mel Lewis, and Clark Terry, and did a great deal of its writing. The band's haunting arrangement of Django Reinhardt's "Manoir de mes rêves" is Bob's.

Bob is a classic illustration of the dictum that jazzmen tend to play pretty much as they speak, which is perhaps inevitable in music that is so extensively improvisatory. He is low-key and quietly ironic in speech, and he plays that way.

But Brookmeyer's main interest for some years now has been composition, and he is an outstanding writer. He had been a founding member in 1965 of the Mel Lewis-Thad Jones Orchestra, which for all that it was a part-time band would become an important finishing school for rising young musicians. After the death of the brilliant Thad Jones in 1986, he became the band's music director and main writer, turning out charts of increasing density and difficulty.

Like Clark Terry and so many jazz musicians, Bob became more and more interested in teaching. In New York in the 1980s he directed a big band workshop for younger arrangers and composers, and then as the nineties dawned he settled in Rotterdam to head a new conservatory devoted to all the arts.

KENNETH VINCENT JOHN (KENNY) WHEELER

Born: Toronto, Ontario, January 14, 1930

As I noted earlier, many relationships in jazz — and no doubt in all the arts — go back far, often to high school years. People are drawn together early by common interests. Kenny Wheeler and I went to high school together. Soon after his family moved to St. Catharines, Ontario, we were introduced in the bedroom of a young mutual friend recently released from a tuberculosis hospital and still resting. The three of us had in common the love of jazz. I was seventeen, Kenny fifteen.

Kenny's father was a part-time trombonist who played in local dance bands. Kenny in those days would do almost anything to gain experience, and he played trumpet in our dreadful high school orchestra during the Wednesday morning assemblies. I suspect that Kenny had a profound influence on me. He turned me on to Sarah Vaughan (for whom I would years later write songs), Miles Davis, and the witty, iconoclastic Sauter-Finegan Orchestra. But I assuredly did not foresee that my painfully reticent young friend would some day occupy a place in the pantheon of major jazz musicians. And he assuredly does, both as a composer and instrumentalist.

At the Toronto Conservatory, Kenny studied harmony with John Weinzweig, the first Canadian composer to practice serial technique. Kenny has often said in interviews that he moved to England (in 1952) at my suggestion, because I recognized that there was at that time little future for an uncompromising jazz musician in Canada. Had he (and I) been able to get visas to the United States, we'd have gone there. Thus I, quite inadvertently, influenced jazz in England and on the Continent, because Kenny became one of the major European jazz figures. His work is now exerting a considerable influence on young players in New York, where he is almost an icon.

The range of Kenny's work is amazing. He has played with Anthony Braxton and George Lewis, Stan Getz, Keith Jarrett, Jack DeJohnette, Dave Holland, and the Clarke-Boland Big Band, the brilliant band based in Cologne and led by drummer Kenny Clarke and the Belgian composer and arranger Francy Boland. Kenny Wheeler is a superb soloist on both trumpet and fluegelhorn. He is also a significant and highly individual composer. His compositions, alas, have been insufficiently recorded. When I received an album of his big band writing in 1989, I put it on the stereo and stopped, in my steps within a few bars. I was startled. Listening to the rest of the record only confirmed my initial impression: this may be genius.

TOMMY LEE FLANAGAN

Born: Detroit, Michigan, March 16, 1930

It has often struck me that musicians who learn another instrument first seem to bring the influence of that instrument to the one on which they finally settle as their life's work. It will probably not surprise you that Oscar Peterson played trumpet as a child, or that Bill Evans played flute and violin. Tommy Flanagan began studying clarinet at the age of six, and I do believe I hear its mellow influence in his lovely, flowing, gracefully legato piano work.

Tommy worked in his early days in Detroit with Milt Jackson and with Thad and Elvin Jones. One of his influences was the third of the Jones brothers, Hank. Others were Bud Powell, Teddy Wilson, and Art Tatum. And after he moved to New York in 1956, Tommy sometimes substituted for Bud Powell at Birdland. In the next few years, he worked with just about everybody of stature in the New York jazz world, including Oscar Pettiford, Miles Davis, J.J. Johnson, Sweets Edison, Sonny Rollins, John Coltrane, and Coleman Hawkins.

Tommy is a soft-spoken and self-effacing man, and one of the gentle and generous accompanists. Ella Fitzgerald hired him as her pianist and music director for many road tours. He worked for her in 1956, from 1963 to '65, and from 1968 to 1978. For a time, in 1966, Tommy was Tony Bennett's music director.

In recent years, he has been working more with small instrumental groups, where his elegant abilities as a soloist are on more advantageous display. Tommy and his wife live in Manhattan.

JAMES STANLEY (JIM) HALL

Born: Buffalo, New York, December 4, 1930

Jim Hall sometimes is compared by critics to Charlie Christian and Django Reinhardt, but then probably every guitarist in jazz has a debt to Christian who, in his short life — he died in 1942 aged twenty-four — became the most important early explorer of amplified guitar as a solo instrument. However, Jim and his trombonist friend Bob Brookmeyer both cite the unsung Jimmy Raney among their influences. From Raney, they say, they developed their integrated and highly compositional approach to the improvised solo, the pensive development of motifs.

Jim started playing guitar professionally in Cleveland when he was in his teens, and he studied at the highly respected Cleveland Institute of Music, from which he received a bachelor of music degree in 1955. He then settled in Los Angeles where he became a member of the Chico Hamilton Quintet, meanwhile studying classical guitar with Vincente Gomez. From 1956 to 1959 he was part of the Jimmy Giuffre Three. Then Jim moved to New York where he was for a time under the curse of his association with so-called West Coast jazz. That ended when one of the major jazz icons, Sonny Rollins, hired him.

Jim had close associations, too, with Paul Desmond, with whom he recorded a series of superb albums for RCA, and with Bill Evans. He and Bill recorded two stunning duo albums together, achieving a rapport that at times was uncanny. Another close associate has been the bassist Ron Carter, with whom he has worked as a duo

from time to time since 1984. He has even recorded with the violinist Itzhak Perlman who, as it happens, is a serious jazz devotee and Art Tatum fan.

Jim is one of the most thoughtful musicians in jazz, and a delight in every context in which he chooses to work. He and his psychotherapist wife Jane live just north of Greenwich Village in Manhattan. Jane is a composer and sometime singer. Jim has recorded some of her tunes.

EDMUND LEONARD (ED) THIGPEN

Born: Chicago, Illinois, December 28, 1930

Edmund Thigpen is yet another example of the way music—as many professions do—runs in families, whether by nature or nurture. He is the son of the late Ben Thigpen, who for seventeen years played drums with Andy Kirk's Clouds of Joy. That's the nature part of it. But Ed's father and mother separated when he was young, and Ed grew up in Los Angeles, where nurture had a lot to do with it, too: Ed went to Jefferson High which produced Art and Addison Farmer, Dexter Gordon, Frank Morgan, Hampton Hawes, and other excellent musicians.

Ed began his professional career as a drummer in the 1950s in the group led by trumpeter Cootie Williams, then went on to work with Dinah Washington, Johnny Hodges, and Lennie Tristano. He recorded extensively, including dates with Art Farmer and John Coltrane, and for a long time he was with the Billy Taylor Trio. While serving in the army, he heard the Oscar Peterson Trio in Tokyo and told himself, "I need to play with this group. I love this group." Ed did join Oscar's group, early in 1959, after Herb Ellis left the trio to settle in Los Angeles, and Oscar decided to replace him not with a guitarist but with a drummer.

Ed stayed with Oscar until 1965. Like Tommy Flanagan, he worked extensively in Ella Fitzgerald's backup group in the 1960s. In 1972 he settled in Copenhagen, which remains his primary home, becoming part of a large contingent of expatriate American jazz musicians who have lived in Europe, among them Ernie Wilkins, Kenny Drew, Red Mitchell, Kenny Clarke, Dexter Gordon, Ben Webster, Don Byas, Bud Powell, Bill Coleman, Sal Nistico, Jiggs Wigham, Sahib Shihab, Sidney Bechet, Steve Lacy, and Art Farmer.

Ed has taught at the Malmö Conservatory in Sweden. He is an outstanding music educator and the author of several books on drums. Oscar Peterson said: "Ed Thigpen is a very reflective yet complete percussionist . . . He had that feeling that it wasn't just drums he was sitting at. He sees his drums as a complete, not instrument, but orchestra. He approaches everything that way."

JOHN (JAKE) HANNA

Born: Boston, Massachusetts, April 4, 1931

Jazz musicians as a group are memorably witty people. Far more so than any group except comedians. It is not a coincidence, then, that quite a number of musicians have crossed the line to become professional comedians, among them Mel Brooks, Jerry Colonna, and Sid Caesar. Trumpeter Jack Sheldon at one point had his own television comedy series. Drummer Jake Hanna's acerbic witticisms are quoted throughout the business. Once Jake was standing by a bar when a woman in her cups was raving rapturously about a conspicuously sloppy jazz trio. After a while Jake said, in a dry delivery that owed not a little to W.C. Fields, "She's made the mistake of drinking on an empty head."

In the early 1960s, when he was the chief propulsive force in the Woody Herman band, Jake used to do a routine, narrated by Woody, that might have been titled *Drummer's Progress*. It was a description of a boy drummer's development from the earliest stage, when he is unable to co-ordinate his hands and feet, through the phases of a career that takes him into such improbably disparate groups as Liberace's and Stan Kenton's. It was hilarious. But it was also a revealing demonstration of versatility, for Jake showed how one could and should play for different people, even if he did it as parody.

That's one reason he is in such demand: adaptability. He is a great big band drummer, and a great trio drummer. At one time Jake played with Marian McPartland and he accompanied Oscar Peterson to the Soviet Union. Versed in every school of jazz, Jake by preference seems to play in a style that recalls the great Swing Era drummers like Jo Jones. He has impeccable time and unfaltering taste, and unless all the musicians around him are disasters, you know this about any group Jake is in: it's going to swing.

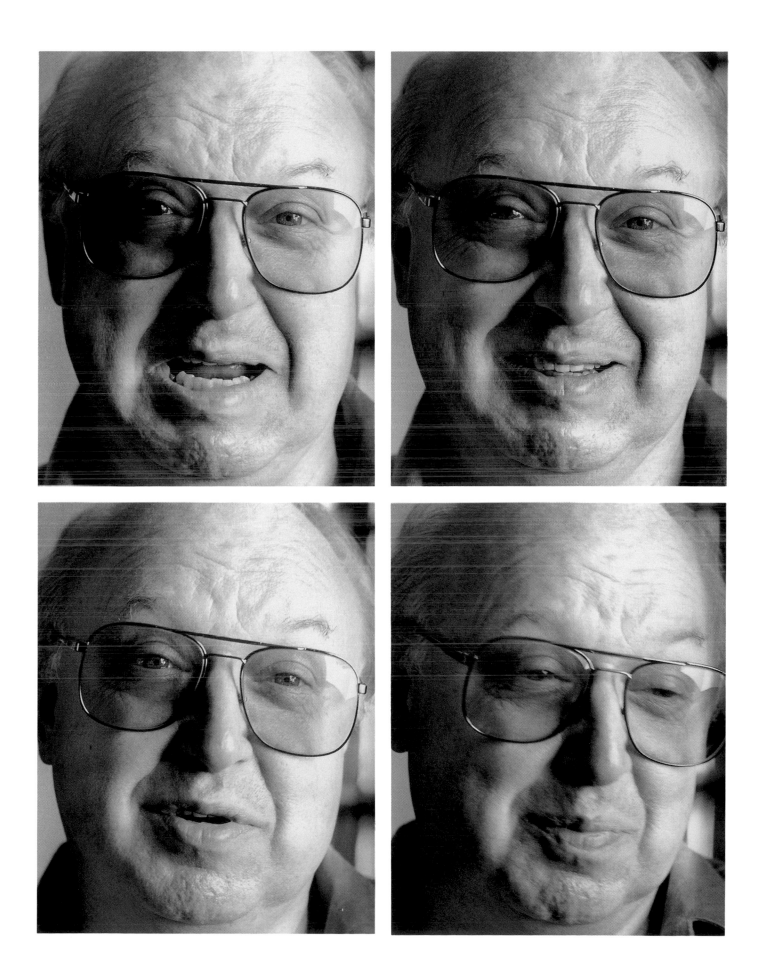

PHILIP WELLS (PHIL) WOODS

Born: Springfield, Massachusetts, November 2, 1931

Phil Woods sometimes refers to himself as Dubois. He is more than half French by ancestry. His father changed the name from Dubois. The rest of Phil is Irish.

When I played one of Phil's records for a friend whose main experience of music was country and western, she said, "Oh yes—he cares." And so he does. Phil's wife Jill (whose brother, Bill Goodwin, is the drummer in Phil's group) once said to me, "Phil's angry about all the right things."

And so he is. He gets angry about indifferent musicianship, politicians, racism, injustice in all its forms, and any failure to render to jazz and its past masters the respect he thinks they deserve. Phil manages to combine in his brilliant alto playing an improbable combination of ferocity and lyricism. Phil once said pointedly that his influences were "Benny Carter, Johnny Hodges, and Charlie Parker, in that order." He has assimilated all his influences to become utterly distinctive, one of those people you can identify in two or three bars, sometimes in one assertive phrase.

Phil graduated from Juilliard as a clarinet major. He still plays the instrument occasionally, and always beautifully. But he has specialized since early days in alto saxophone, on which he achieves a huge tone. He has played with absolutely everybody of consequence in jazz, in every imaginable context, and has recorded with Benny Carter and Dizzy Gillespie, two of his major heroes. He is an intriguing composer and, as a soloist, inexhaustibly inventive.

One of Phil's early idols was Artie Shaw, on whose work he modeled his own clarinet playing. It was my pleasure to introduce Phil to Artie, who began his professional career on saxophone, at a party after one of Phil's concerts. Also at that party was the fine tenor saxophone player Eddie Miller. When Phil had gone off in the crowd of his admirers, Shaw said to me, "I've heard them all. All. Phil Woods is the best saxophone player I ever heard." And Eddie Miller warmly agrees.

Phil is completely uncompromising. He dislikes amplification, and will not allow microphones on the bandstand. Though he was a successful studio musician in New York in the 1960s, he has since then declined to play anything but jazz, and only on his terms. He tours with a quintet that usually contains a second horn, whether trumpet or trombone. Tom Harrell is one of the alumni of his group.

I don't wish to make Phil sound forbidding. He isn't. Indeed, he's terribly funny and a delight to be with. But Jill got it right; I know no one on this earth with more integrity than Philip Wells Woods.

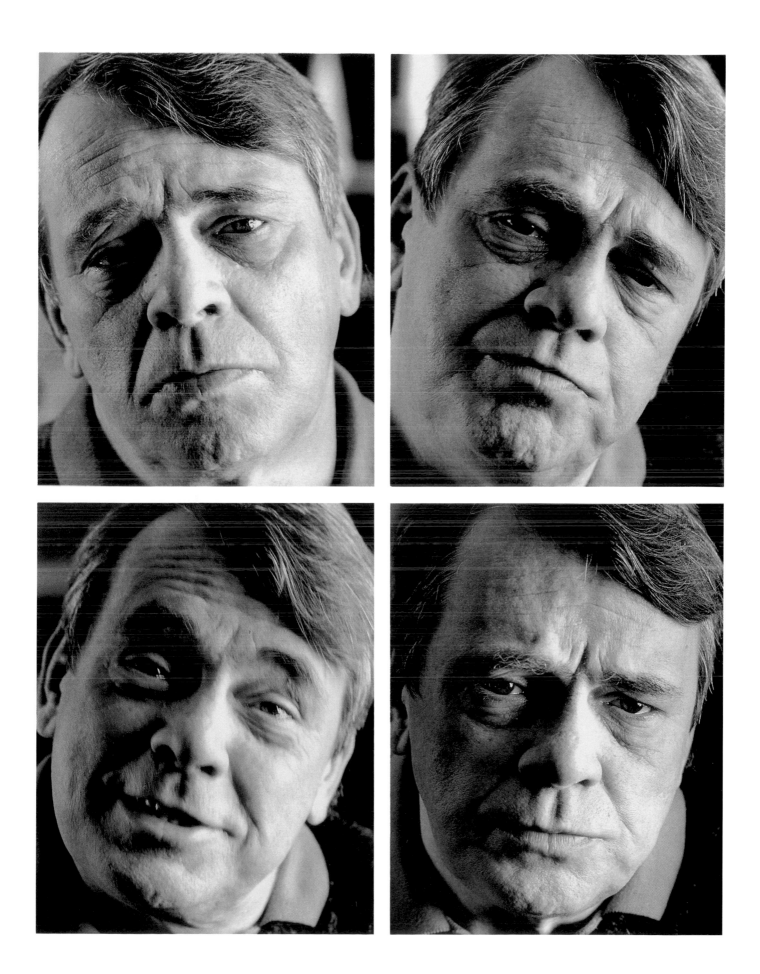

EDWARD ISAAC (ED) BICKERT

Born: Hochfield, Manitoba, November 29, 1932

Some time in the early 1970s, when I was living in Toronto, alto saxophonist Paul Desmond called me from New York. He had been asked to play a Toronto club and wanted to know what I thought. I urged him to do it.

"But what will I do for a rhythm section?" he asked. I told him to get a bass player named Don Thompson, either Terry Clarke or Jerry Fuller on drums, and a guitar player named Ed Bickert. "Oh yes," Paul said, "Jim Hall told me about him. Jim said he's the one guy who scares him if he walks into the room when Jim's playing."

Paul came, saw, and was conquered, and thereafter recorded a number of times with Ed, Don, and Jerry. In the liner notes to one of their albums, Paul wrote: "I find myself turning around . . . to count the strings on [Bickert's] guitar . . . I'm reasonably sure that it's less than eighty-eight."

As it happened, Ed told Paul, when he was learning guitar in his home on the Canadian prairies he had listened to early 1950s broadcasts from San Francisco by the Dave Brubeck Quartet with Desmond.

Ed is remarkable for the extraordinary technique that he uses in deceptively unprepossessing fashion. Because it is a fretted instrument, the guitar has inherent intonation problems. It is even a nuisance to tune. But Ed's intonation is so accurate that, according to members of Rob McConnell's Boss Brass, the band tunes up to him.

Ed is taciturn. Usually he sits on the bandstand with a cigarette hanging from the corner of his mouth, taking in the world around him. But he can talk when he wants to, volubly and articulately. I once did an interview with him. Next day I told the guys in the Boss Brass, "You won't believe what I got on tape yesterday. An *hour* of Ed Bickert *talking*."

Since Desmond first stood there open-mouthed over Ed's playing, Ed has recorded with all sorts of major players and groups, including the Boss Brass, of which he was a founding member, Benny Carter, and Oscar Peterson. He has recorded with his own groups and toured extensively.

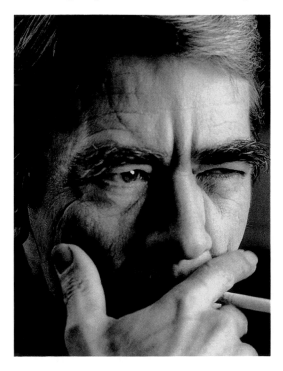

DONALDSON TOUSSAINT L'OUVERTURE (DONALD) BYRD

Born: Detroit, Michigan, December 9, 1932

Nowadays they call them magnet schools. But there have always been high schools that produced outstanding jazz players. Cass Tech in Detroit produced all sorts of talent in many fields; jazz is just one of them. Cass Tech gave the world Pepper Adams, Yusef Lateef, Frank Rosolino, and Donald Byrd.

Donald — his middle names commemorate the revolutionary leader who expelled the French from Haiti in 1804 — attended Wayne State, then earned a bachelor of music and a master's from the Manhattan School in New York. He went across the street to Columbia University, where he picked up two more degrees. But his real finishing schools were the groups of Art Blakey and Horace Silver.

Byrd was considered the heir apparent to Clifford Brown after Brown's death in 1956. He played trumpet in a soaring, strong style with a tone, he once told me, that derived directly from symphonic brass playing. He and his friend, baritone saxophonist Pepper Adams, co-led a quintet between 1958 and 1961. One day Donald brought to my apartment in Chicago a young pianist he had hired right out of college. One constantly reads that Miles Davis was the first to discover this young man. He wasn't; Donald was. The pianist's name was Herbie Hancock.

Donald has an abiding passion for education. He studied composition in Europe in 1962 and '63, and taught at the Stan Kenton band camps, as well as at Rutgers University, the Hampton Institute, Howard University, and North Carolina Uni-

versity. In 1976 he even got a law degree and, in 1982, a doctorate from Columbia University Teachers College.

Brilliantly intelligent, deeply thoughtful and analytical, Byrd has a wonderful way with students. You can sit there and watch the admiration in their eyes. His past students include saxophonists Chris Hollyday and Antonio Hart, and trumpeters Roy Hargrove and Darren Barrett.

Donald now heads the jazz program at the New School for Social Research and is a full professor at Brooklyn's Queens College, whose jazz program he established.

CEDAR ANTHONY WALTON, JR.

Born: Dallas, Texas, January 17, 1934

Cedar Walton's childhood passed in an atmosphere of racial pressure. The pressure did not let up when he went to Dillard University in New Orleans, where a fellow student was Ellis Marsalis, later to be a respected music educator and father of the famous Marsalis brothers. It didn't end until Cedar moved on to the music school of the University of Denver.

"Denver's quiet," he said, "it's not like Texas. There was a pressure lifted. It's not as blunt as in Texas. I grew up with the signs on the bus. You know, you had to sit behind them. So that was something I found removed. By this time I had learned to be terrified by white people, in a sense. But I worked it out. I'm talking about 1951 or '52. 'Afraid' isn't entirely accurate. But there was a hesitancy on my part, simply because I just wasn't used to it. It's like going into a cage of lions. You're a lion yourself, but you've never been around

that breed of lion. But I got used to it. I could relate to the instructors. It turned me, I think, into a fanatic student in terms of trying to keep up. I zeroed in on my music." Before he was twenty, Cedar was playing piano in a Denver club. One night Charlie Parker came by and sat in. Like everyone who had these chance encounters with Parker, Cedar never forgot it. He shortly met Dizzy Gillespie, and Johnny Hodges, and John Coltrane.

Leaving the University of Denver after three years, Cedar went to New York where he became yet another of the alumni of Art Blakey: he recorded with everybody, replaced McCoy Tyner in the Art Farmer-Benny Golson Jazztet, and established himself as one of the finest pianists in the post-bop idiom. Today Cedar devotes himself to composing, and recording as a leader. He lives near the ocean in Brentwood, California, and travels constantly.

SHIRLEY HORN

Born: Washington, DC, May 1, 1934

It would seem that there have been far more women singers in jazz who play piano than male singers who do — Jeri Southern, Sarah Vaughan, Audrey Morris, Carmen McRae, Blossom Dearie, and Shirley Horn among them. Why this should be so is uncertain. Perhaps it's that men who play piano are allowed to do only that, while women are *expected* to sing as well; it's a "feminine" thing to do. Men have always had trouble accepting women as jazz instrumentalists. So what do you do with them? Have them sing. That all the aforementioned play piano well is obscured by the high quality of their singing. And Shirley Horn is a really superb pianist, so much so that when Carmen McRae went into the studio in 1990 to record an album in tribute to her late friend Sarah Vaughan, she had Shirley as her accompanist. The two then made plans to record an album with Shirley singing and Carmen playing piano.

Shirley started studying piano at the age of four, and continued those studies into her years at Howard University in Washington, D.C. She won a scholarship to Juilliard but could not accept it because her family didn't have the money to let her go to New York. At twenty she began leading her own trio and singing with it, soon attracting the notice of Miles Davis and other significant jazz musicians. This led to a good deal of recording, all of it at a high level. But Shirley had married and wanted to raise her family. She withdrew from the travel and bustle of the music business, confining her activities to the Washington area. Then in the 1980s she began to record again, to enormous critical acclaim. Miles Davis made one of his last recordings backing her in a great album of standards.

Unlike a number of jazz singers who have a knowledge of harmony, Shirley doesn't assault a song. She sings softly and without strain, always in deep contact with the meanings of words. And she is a superb accompanist to herself, playing with a rich warm tone and lovely chord voicings. As the 1990s began, Shirley was in demand at jazz festivals. I saw her one night at Hollywood Bowl on a program opposite Dave Brubeck. She held that vast outdoor audience in mesmerized attention, as if that airy amphitheater were her own living room.

ROBERT MURRAY GORDON (ROB) MCCONNELL

Born: London, Ontario, Canada, February 14, 1935

In 1977 a two-record set called *Big Band Jazz* came out of Toronto. Soon arrangers and composers around the world owned it. The album was by the Boss Brass. The level of performing was electrifying. The ensemble playing was impeccable, and it seemed every man in the band, Ed Bickert among them, was a major soloist. What made it all work was the writing of the band's leader, Rob McConnell.

That album established Rob as a major international figure among jazz composers. When Rob and the Boss Brass went to California to play a week at Donte's, the place was packed with the best of the Los Angeles musicians. Conspicuous among them were composers including Pete Rugolo and Henry Mancini. A long series of albums followed, including one with Phil Woods as guest. In 1992 the band was still going strong, with a personnel roster that had hardly changed in twenty years.

We have noted the influence of certain high school band programs and teachers on jazz in the United States. In 1928 in Vancouver, British Columbia, an English cornetist and bandmaster named Arthur Delamont formed the Kitsilano Boys' Band, which toured as far as the USSR and turned out a large number of the best Canadian brass players, including Arnie Chykoski, the stunning lead trumpeter of the Boss Brass. And he turned out his own son, Gordon Delamont, who, while never very successful as a composer himself, had a far-reaching influence through his textbooks and the musicians he trained, among them Moe Koffman and Rob

McConnell. Rob's writing, like that of Gil Evans and other innovators, is much imitated, including a device of having the brass or reed sections play soli while the rhythm section lays out.

For three years Rob held a job in a brokerage house, and for a while he fed his young family by working in a gas station. But the lure of music was too strong. He switched from slide to valve trombone, worked in dance bands, and made the inevitable pilgrimage to New York, where he played in the Maynard Ferguson band in 1964. He received an invitation to replace Bob Brookmeyer in the Gerry Mulligan Quartet, and later returned to Toronto to become one of the stalwarts of the commercial recording business. Gifted, or cursed, with an acerbic wit, Rob was liable to tell a producer what he really thought of the music in an advertising jingle. This in time left him with little choice but to form the Boss Brass. The band has recorded more than twenty albums, one of which, *All in Good Time*, won a Grammy in 1983.

In view of the influence of Percy Faith, Robert Farnon, Kenny Wheeler, and Gil Evans, all Toronto natives, and latterly that of Rob, who grew up in Toronto, the city takes on a surprising significance in jazz composition.

HERBERT LAWRENCE GREENIDGE (SONNY GREENWICH)

Born: Hamilton, Ontario, January 1, 1936

Sonny Greenwich is one of the best-kept secrets in jazz. A highly original guitarist who incorporates into his work stylistic influences as disparate as Sonny Rollins and Maria Callas, he has removed himself from view, and even from playing, for long periods of time. William Faulkner used to say that he was not a literary man. Sonny Greenwich told an interviewer, "I'm not a working musician. When I decide to play, I play to awake people spiritually — that's the only reason." The extended sabbaticals are the result of his deep spiritual interests, and a recurring illness of which he has absolutely refused to speak publicly beyond saying that when it affects him it drains him of energy.

He became interested in the guitar in his late teens when his father, a pianist, presented him with one. In his early twenties he worked in a rhythm and blues band, playing Toronto bars and strip joints, then various jazz clubs. A meeting with John Coltrane in Buffalo reinforced his spiritual leanings, and strongly influenced his emerging playing style. In 1966-67 he toured with the San Francisco-based saxophonist John Handy, whose group included two other Canadians, drummer Terry Clarke and pianist-bassist-vibraharpist Don Thompson. He toured briefly with saxophonist Hank Mobley, then, in a New York engagement in 1968, led a group that included bassist Jimmy Garrison and drummer Jack DeJohnette. He worked briefly with Miles Davis in 1969. Greenwich then recorded in Toronto with a group he co-led with Don Thompson, all

the while turning down offers from leaders as important as drummer Elvin Jones and vibraharpist Gary Burton. He moved to the Montreal area in 1967, and still lives there with his wife Catherine, a dancer.

Sonny Rollins withdrew from the profession for a time. He would go out on one of the New York bridges at night and play. Sonny Greenwich used to take his guitar into a Toronto park deep in the night, keeping an eye out for the cops. "I'd go out there and play toward the stars."

On another occasion he said, "I feel that the space between my hands is God, that everything is God, and I've been trying to get closer and closer to this idea of unity, people and love, and this is the basis for all my music."

BILLY HIGGINS

Born: Los Angeles, California, October 11, 1936

Most musicians dislike categories and pigeonholes and often rebel against them. Billy Higgins has simply ignored them. He began his career in his native city drumming in rhythm and blues and rock bands, performing with Amos Milburn and Bo Diddley, among others. He then played in the Jazz Messiahs, a group co-led by trumpeter Don Cherry and saxophonist James Clay, and with saxophonist Dexter Gordon.

During the late 1950s, he took part in rehearsals with iconoclastic saxophonist Ornette Coleman, thus becoming a charter member of Coleman's famous group. He performed in New York with Coleman's quartet during the period when it was perplexing the jazz establishment and harvesting the praise of such figures as Leonard Bernstein.

No sooner was Higgins perceived as a drummer of the avant-garde than he established his credentials as a great player in more traditional forms, recording with Donald Byrd, Sonny Clark, Clifford Jordan, Hank Mobley, Lee Morgan, Jackie McLean, Mal Waldron, and many more — a drummer for all seasons and all situations, always with superb taste and a relaxed, irresistible swing.

He has continued to record in all sorts of contexts, working with Milt Jackson, Art Pepper, J.J. Johnson, Joe Henderson, Pat Metheny, Cedar Walton, and Slide Hampton. Indeed he is considered one of the most recorded drummers in jazz.

Billy still lives in Los Angeles.

EDDIE HARRIS

Born: Chicago, Illinois, October 20, 1936

The late Bud Freeman, a native of Chicago and one of that city's most ardent loyalists, argued that jazz was invented not in New Orleans but in Chicago. It's debatable, of course, but if you accept that jazz is an art of stellar improvising soloists, then Bud had a point, because it was in Chicago that Louis Armstrong and Earl Hines and Jimmie Noone and Bix Beiderbecke and Benny Goodman (only Goodman a native) matured and honed their craft, and set the direction of the music.

I lived in Chicago from 1959 to 1962, the period when I was editor of *Down Beat,* and the city was (as it is now) an extraordinarily fertile garden of jazz, madly florid with talents both native and imported. Eddie Harris was one of the natives. He was unknown outside the city at that time. I have delightful memories of cruising from one club to another with Eddie to visit our friends. I thought he was an outstanding musician, an original composer, and a fine player on several instruments. He was fascinated by all sorts of sonorities, experimenting with trombone fitted with reed mouthpieces, tenor saxophone fitted with trombone mouthpiece, and more. He'd show me these tricks at his house, and we'd laugh. Tenor, though, was his main instrument. He made an album for the small Chicago label called Veejay. One of the tunes he recorded was the theme from the film *Exodus*, which became a huge hit, and launched Eddie as a national and later international name.

Eddie moved to Los Angeles and recorded with all manner of the best jazz musicians. In 1969 he teamed up with pianist and singer Les McCann. They gave a performance at the Montreux Jazz Festival, the recording of which cranked both their careers a notch higher.

Eddie once told me that he had asked the great tenor saxophonist Lester Young a question about embouchure. Pres told him, "I can only tell you about *my* mouthpiece in *my* mouth. I can't tell you about *your* mouthpiece in *your* mouth."

Eddie used to improvise satires on the blues as we'd ride around Chicago in his car, laughter trailing in the night.

HERBERT RICHARD (RICK) WILKINS

Born: Hamilton, Ontario, February 1, 1937

I first encountered Rick's music in 1970 in Switzerland, at the Golden Rose television festival, which is dedicated to TV musical specials. The Canadian Broadcasting Corporation had submitted a broadcast, a very humorous one. What struck me most, however, was the quality of the big-band jazz writing heard throughout it. I made a special note of the arranger's name: Rick Wilkins. Long afterwards I found out that he, like Sonny Greenwich, was born in the same city I was, and that his birthday is exactly a week after mine — make of that what you will. I have since then had the privilege of hearing some of my music arranged and conducted by Rick, an experience I found quite unforgettable. I even wrote a song with him once.

Rick started out writing in Hamilton for dance bands. In 1957 he moved to Toronto, where he studied arranging for a short time with Phil Nimmons at the Advanced School of Contemporary Music headed by Oscar Peterson. He has written extensively in television, in both Toronto and Los Angeles. Rick is some writer.

He is also some tenor player, a fact that was obscured for a time by his prominence as an arranger and composer. That has been corrected in recent years, and indeed there are jazz fans in other countries who know him now chiefly for his tenor work. Rather taciturn in most social situations, Rick is an exception to the rule that jazz musicians play as they speak. His big, strong, extraverted tenor sound, one of the important voices of the Boss Brass — for which he writes as well as plays — is at variance with his low, soft, diffident manner of speech.

CHARLES EDWARD (CHARLIE) HADEN

Born: Shenandoah, Iowa, August 6, 1937

Charlie Haden's father, Carl Haden, was a country and western musician who played guitar and harmonica and sang on radio stations, at county fairs, and in evangelists' tents throughout Kansas, Iowa, and Oklahoma. Charlie was steeped in the music of his father's friends, including Jimmy Rogers and the Carter family. Charlie's professional career began when he was only twenty-two months old: he sang on a radio program. All Charlie's relatives sang and played washboards and jugs, among them his grandfather, Buster Haden, who played the fiddle on his chest. Charlie's grandmother remembered both Wild Bill Hickock and Jesse James.

Charlie got interested in jazz in high school, through his brother. "The harmonies of jazz really attracted me," Charlie says. "The dissonance and the counterpoint and the unusual intervals. I loved it." Charlie learned to read music, went on to serious formal study, some of it at the Westlake School of Music in California, and evolved into one of the most versatile bass players in jazz, with a range of interests and tastes running across the whole spectrum of jazz. He was a member of the radical Ornette Coleman Quintet which shook the jazz world in the early 1960s.

He has led his own Liberation Music Orchestra as well as a quartet with Alan Broadbent on piano, Ernie Watts on tenor saxophone, and Billy Higgins (his old associate from the Ornette Coleman group) on drums.

"The great thing about this art form," Charlie says, "is that musicians care about beautiful sound. They want to make their instruments sound really, really beautiful. It's so important, beautiful sound — to be able to hear the beauty of the musician's soul . . . It's a dedication and honesty you don't find very many places. Improvisation and spontaneity are about honesty. The musician is baring his soul to the people, and hoping he can touch their lives, in a humble way. Every great musician learns that before you can become a great musician, you have to become a good human being."

GUIDO BASSO

Born: Montreal, Quebec, September 27, 1937

Sometimes great technicians are not warm players. Guido is an outstanding exception. He was a child prodigy on trumpet, which he studied (as did Maynard Ferguson) at the Conservatoire de musique de Montréal. He played in Montreal dance bands in his teens, then was hired at eighteen to go on the road with singer Vic Damone. From 1957 to 1960 he was a member of the Louie Bellson band, which backed Pearl Bailey, Bellson's wife. In 1960 he moved to Toronto, where he became a top studio musician, leader, television music director, and recording artist. He led the orchestra on two Canadian Broadcasting Corporation TV series devoted to big bands, and in 1973 organized big bands for Toronto appearances by Benny Goodman, Duke Ellington, and Dizzy Gillespie.

Guido was one of the charter members of the Boss Brass, whose albums heavily feature his soaring, romantically warm fluegelhorn solos. He spins seemingly endless lines which raise you to pinnacles of suspense as you wonder if he's ever going to take a breath.

Guido has done his fair share of studio dates, enduring with good grace the boredom of playing music designed to sell soup and soap. Having put aside enough money to let him do just what wants to do, he plans to follow the path of Bud Shank and Herb Ellis: go back to his great love, playing jazz.

Some years ago an exchange took place between Guido and Johnny Audino, one of the great trumpet players in the Los Angeles studio world. Both, of course, are of Italian background. Guido said to Johnny, "Do you realize that in Toronto we now have 500,000 Italians?" And Johnny snapped back, "Do you realize that in Los Angeles we have 500,000 Italian *musicians?*"

JOHN HEARD

Born: Pittsburgh, Pennsylvania, July 3, 1938

John Heard is one of the great bass players. He is also a photographer and painter who specializes in portraits. For a while he even tried to give up music for this other talent.

John grew up in a district of Pittsburgh called Manchester which, he says, was so dangerous that some people declined to set foot in it. In those days there was so much air pollution from the steel mills that sometimes the street lamps would be lit in the daytime. A speech impediment — John stammers, and tells you so immediately — caused him to be teased cruelly in his childhood. He learned to fight in his own defense; John is both tall and genuinely tough. For all that he is also a warm and humorous man.

He spent a period of his youth in the U.S. Air Force, stationed in Germany. There he made money on the side painting portraits of officers and teaching art to their wives. He'd use his spare time to go to Paris to hear pianist Bud Powell and visit the Louvre. "The *Mona Lisa*," he said. "The minute I saw it I got goose pimples. It blew me away. Also in Paris I was very impressed by the Impressionists, Degas and Monet in particular. And I loved Van Gogh."

When John got out of service in 1962, he went to work as a bass player, and gradually built a name through his work with Jon Hendricks, Ahmad Jamal, Count Basie, and Oscar Peterson. "John Heard," Oscar said, "is a watershed bass player."

He has a very individual approach to the instrument, producing a long loping arc between the beats. I can spot John instantly on a record. He is the only bassist I ever heard who could alter the feel of the Basie rhythm section. I just love his playing. And his portrait of Ella Fitzgerald hangs in my living room.

WARREN BERNHARDT

Born: Wausau, Wisconsin, November 13, 1938

When I first met Warren Bernhardt in a Chicago club, he was still a chemist. He had a phenomenal Oscar Peterson-like technique on piano. I couldn't understand why anyone with that kind of musical talent could possibly want to devote his life to anything else, and I encouraged him to make music his profession.

Warren, whose father was also a pianist, had grown up surrounded by the major concert pianists of the era, including Rudolph Serkin. Warren played his first classical concert when he was nine. When he was ten, Serkin invited him to come to live and study with him. Warren declined, because he didn't want to give up his baseball games with schoolmates.

Not long after our first meeting, in 1963, Warren and I traveled for six months all through Latin America, almost as far south as Tierra del Fuego. He was the pianist in the Paul Winter Sextet, while I managed the group's State Department tour. I carried a small portable stereo set with two sets of headphones, and Warren and I — when we weren't working — were constantly listening to Bill Evans. I particularly remember our being enraptured by Bill's "Haunted Heart" in an old hotel in Belém as we looked out across the vast Amazon River.

Later, in New York, we shared an apartment for a while, and I introduced him to a lot of my friends, including Gerry Mulligan and Bill Evans.

Warren worked in New York with Clark Terry, Gerry Mulligan, Mike Mainieri, Jack DeJohnette, Jeremy Steig, Tim Har-din, Jimmy Cobb, Richie Havens, Liza Minnelli, and Carly Simon, and he was a member of one of the jazz "super groups" of the eighties, Steps Ahead.

Now Warren and his wife live a quiet life in a big house near Bearsville, New York, not far from Woodstock. Jack DeJohnette is a neighbor.

I don't think he's had the full recognition he deserves. Some people have noticed, though. A French journalist wrote, "At the top of the mountain, deep in the pool of great genius where Bill Evans lives, there also lives Warren Bernhardt."

ALFRED MCCOY TYNER

Born: Philadelphia, Pennsylvania, December 11, 1938

I wrote earlier of the strong regional characteristics and loyalties in jazz. Just as John Heard can rattle off the names of those great musicians born in Pittsburgh and Donald Byrd will tell you who was born in Detroit, so can Philadelphia jazz people recite the list of those born there: Donald Bailey, Kenny Barron, Joe Beck, Mike and Randy Brecker, Ray Bryant, Stanley Clarke, Warren Covington, Ted Curson, Spanky De Brest, Bill Doggett, Ziggy Elman, Stan Getz, Benny Golson, Bill Harris, Tootie and Jimmy Heath, Gregory Herbert, Philly Joe Jones, Billy Kyle, Eddie Lang, John LaPorta, Jimmy McGriff, Lee Morgan, Paul Motian, Tommy Potter, Luckey Roberts, Red Rodney, Jimmy Rowser, Rex Stewart, Lew Tabackin, Bobby Timmons, Charlie Ventura, Jimmy Woode, Reggie Workman — and McCoy Tyner. And they're proud of it.

When Benny Golson formed the Jazztet with Art Farmer in 1962, Benny sent for a home boy to play piano. It was McCoy's first national exposure, and he made quite a splash. This edition of the Jazztet lasted a year and a half. From that group, McCoy was offered the piano chair in the quartet John Coltrane was organizing. Though Coltrane was not born in Philadelphia, he spent his formative adolescent years there, and all these youngbloods knew each other. Indeed Coltrane and McCoy, like Red Rodney, had both studied at the Granoff School of Music. The drummer in Coltrane's new group was Elvin Jones, the bassist Jimmy Garrison. It was a group that would cast a very long shadow. McCoy stayed with it from 1960 to 1965.

In the middle and latter 1960s, McCoy made a series of superb records for the Impulse and Blue Note labels, further establishing himself as an innovative composer as well as an incredibly powerful, driving, dazzling, and original pianist. Those records sound as fresh today as when they were made.

As the 1980s ended, McCoy was back at Blue Note, playing as strongly as ever.

"All music," McCoy says, "is a journey of the soul into new, uncharted territory."

WILLIAM RUSSELL (BILL) WATROUS II

Born: Middletown, Connecticut, June 8, 1939

From the late 1940s through the end of the 1960s, there was a restaurant and bar on West 48th Street called Jim and Andy's. It was the most popular of the four New York watering holes favored by musicians. Famous faces were to be found there every day and evening, and when a newcomer turned up, he was noticed.

The fresh young face of trombonist Bill Watrous first appeared there in 1961. A story rapidly made the rounds at J&A's, as the place was usually called. It seems Bill got a job on a session with one of his idols, the revered J.J. Johnson. Bill proceeded to play, as a tribute, one of J.J.'s recorded solos note for note. J.J. was astounded, and Bill was established. "I didn't do it to show off," he said long afterwards. "I did it to Urbie Green and Jimmy Cleveland too. It was an act of love for their work."

Jazz pushed out the frontiers of almost every instrument its practitioners chose to play, extending the technical range far beyond what was expected in the world of classical music. And no instrument was as revolutionized as the trombone, which in symphony orchestras and brass bands had been confined to oom-pah roles and occasional simple melodies such as the theme of the Ravel *Bolero*. Jazz influenced the way symphony trombonists now play.

Jack Teagarden established as far back as the 1920s that trombone could be played with a speed and facility close to that of trumpet. Tommy Dorsey, who never even looked on himself as a great jazz player, expanded the tessitura — the natural range of an instrument or voice — far upward, and played with a seamless lyrical fluency. And then came J.J. Johnson, who brought bebop to the horn and played the instrument with speed and powers of invention that took everyone's breath away. After that, the deluge, as a whole generation of brilliant trombonists such as Frank Rosolino, Jimmy Cleveland, and Curtis Fuller made what had been the impossible into the norm for the instrument.

Then came Bill Watrous. At first he was known as a master technician. But as the years went on, I watched Bill grow into an artist, a player of great beauty and sensitivity. Now he has become an influence on other trombonists. In the early seventies he formed his own big band, Manhattan Wildlife Refuge.

ROGER KELLAWAY

Born: Waban, Massachusetts, November 1, 1939

No one has had as much influence on my musical thinking as Roger Kellaway. When you write songs together, and Roger and I have been doing that for nearly twenty years, you get to know how your associate's mind works.

Once we were at a party at Henry Mancini's house. Roger was playing piano. Hank listened, shook his head in admiration of Kellaway's protean and unorthodox gifts, grinned, and said, "Roger, you're crazy."

No one I know can work in so many styles. He's recorded with everyone of note in jazz. One song Roger and I wrote had a simple country and western style melody. Yet Roger is an established and highly respected symphonic composer. His jazz playing can be poignantly lyrical or rhythmically powerful, and when it's the latter there is a certain wildness in it, for Roger has a taste and talent for poly-

tonality. His hands have an astonishing rhythmic independence. Roger's iconoclastic Cello Quartet records, with an instrumentation of cello, bass, percussion, and piano, are now considered classics.

Roger is a product of the New England Conservatory in Boston. He worked professionally as a bass player as well as a pianist, and sang in the conservatory chorus, on one occasion under Charles Munch. His tastes run all the way from the earliest music to the most experimental. For all the scope of his accomplishments, Roger sometimes has attacks of the uncertainty that plague all artists. Once we attended a rehearsal of the music he wrote for a George Balanchine ballet. He asked me to tape it for him. Later we sat in his car and listened, and at the end he said with a sort of sigh, "Well, I guess I do have some talent."

DONALD WINSTON (DON) THOMPSON

Born: Powell River, British Columbia, January 18, 1940

John Heard told me that one of the bass players who had a formative influence on him was Don Thompson. This was during the mid-1960s, when they were both living in San Francisco. Don lived there while touring with the John Handy Quintet (whose drummer was Terry Clarke) from 1965 to 1967. In 1969 he moved to Toronto, which remains his home.

Paul Desmond had two especially favorite bass players. Ron Carter was one, Don was the other. Together, Paul and Don recorded quite a number of albums. Don has worked in a duo with Jim Hall who, interestingly, often does duo concerts with Ron Carter. He's recorded with people as disparate as pianist Jay McShann and saxophonist Dave Liebman, and he has worked extensively with George Shearing, traveling all over the world with him. But there was a twist to the Shearing duo. Shearing discovered that Don is a superb pianist as well, and in concerts they would usually do a piano duo segment.

That's not the end of it. Don is an outstanding vibraharp player too. And he has at one time or another played other instruments. He's also a recording engineer and producer. For all this astonishing musicianship, he told me, "I don't feel competent to teach any instrument. I only teach music."

Along with Kenny Wheeler, Don has taught for some years at the Banff Centre in Alberta, Canada. In the nearest I have ever heard Don come to boasting, he told me that about 75 percent of the best youngblood players in Canada today had passed through their tutelage.

Tall, bearded, with the serious mien of a preoccupied prophet, Don is deceptive. The first time one of his sardonic witticisms comes your way you think you must have heard wrong. You didn't. Don is one of the funniest persons you'll ever meet.

In 1990, Don recorded an album with Kenny Wheeler. All the pieces were Thompson compositions. On that one Don played piano; Dave Holland played bass. Don is another charter member of the Boss Brass. He was first its percussonist, then bassist; now he's the pianist.

ADAM MAKOWICZ

Born: Gnojnik, Czechoslovakia, August 18, 1940

One of the unsung heroes of jazz history is a U.S. broadcaster and jazz authority named Willis Conover, whose name is known in every country in the world but his own. Yet Conover singlehandedly made jazz an international musical language through his *Music USA* broadcasts. Speaking slowly so that those with little English could follow him, Conover introduced the music to people everywhere, inspiring countless musicians to learn to play it.

One of these was Adam Makowicz (pronounced Ma-KO-vitch), born in Czechoslovakia of Polish parents. The family returned to Poland shortly after the Second World War, and Adam grew up in Katowice, the capital of Silesia. He started studying music at the age of nine, and was headed for a career as a concert pianist. Enter Willis Conover. Adam remembers: "Nobody knew about jazz at that time. Besides it was banned from public life. It was illegal music under the Nazis and under Stalin. My friends from music school told me about *Music USA*, which we could get on short wave radio. It was *Music USA*'s Jazz Hour from Voice of America. It was the only source to learn about jazz. I was seventeen or eighteen when I started to play jazz in student clubs and the homes of friends.

"Art Tatum was, musically speaking, like my father. When I heard his music for the first time, and each time was like the first time, he really turned me on. And this feeling has not diminished. I still admire him, and I still say he is the greatest all-time jazz pianist who ever lived. He was using the whole keyboard all the time."

Record producer John Hammond heard some of Adam's early recordings. Benny Goodman was about to visit Poland. Hammond asked Goodman, who was married to Hammond's sister, to listen to the pianist and seek out more of his records. After hearing them, Hammond brought Adam to the United States and in 1977 recorded him for Columbia Records. Adam and his wife, Irena, decided to settle in New York.

Adam has turned out a series of records that can only be called astonishing. Gifted with a fertile imagination and an unlimited technique, he is not only an extraordinary pianist, he is also a fascinating composer.

In 1991, he returned to a Poland he had at one time thought he would never see again. He toured the country triumphantly for a month, playing an all-Gershwin program that included two of the *Preludes* and, with the Great Symphony Orchestra of the National Philharmonic, *Rhapsody in Blue*.

On his return to America, Adam was awarded a grant from the National Endowment for the Arts to perform three concerts in tribute to Art Tatum — in New York, Washington, D.C., and Toledo, Ohio. Why Toledo? Art Tatum was born there.

JACK DeJOHNETTE

Born: Chicago, Illinois, August 9, 1942

It is common for jazz musicians who play other instruments to play at least a little piano as well, if only out of the need to know harmony. Dizzy Gillespie plays good piano, although you'll never hear him do it in public. The late drummer Philly Joe Jones played piano very well. Rarely, however, do players known for other instruments play piano as well as Jack DeJohnette, an innovative and enormously influential drummer. Jack was trained as a concert pianist, starting when he was four and studying for ten years. An uncle who was a disc jockey got him interested in jazz, and he took up drums when he was about eighteen. Another Chicagoan, Eddie Harris, for whom Jack worked, urged him to make it his main instrument. "You've got to make up your mind which one you're gonna play," Eddie said. "You've got to make your mark on one. You play good piano, but drums, I'll tell you, if you stick with drums, you're gonna make a lot of money."

Jack says that one of his important influences was the Bill Evans Trio with Paul Motian on drums and Scott LaFaro on bass. Moving to New York, he worked with John Coltrane, Stan Getz, Jackie McLean, the Charles Lloyd Quartet — and the Bill Evans Trio, whose bassist then was Eddie Gomez. In 1969, Jack join the Miles Davis Quintet, recording the important album *Bitches Brew* with the group.

Jack and his artist wife, who has designed some of his album covers, live in a "rustic modern" house near Woodstock, New York. Neighbors include Warren Bernhardt and bassist Dave Holland.

When John Reeves and I visited Jack, the Gulf War, with attendant frenzied American jingoism, was under way. This had put Jack in a pensive mood. He told us, "The great American experiment cannot be said to have failed, because the great American experiment remains to be completed."

And of jazz he said, "After John Coltrane died, the spiritual aspect of the music went out the window. That's the element I hope we get back to, because we do need a spiritual renaissance. We have *work* to do. *How* we work is what matters.

"In our computer age, we have to learn to sort out valuable information from nonsense, from the trivial. We have to then learn how to slow down and let things take their time to build. There is too much expectation on young musicians, writers, poets, playwrights, dancers, all artists who haven't had time yet to build."

One young musician whom Jack is helping to build is the eighteen-year-old trumpeter Ryan Kisor, formerly of Sioux City, Iowa. Jack produced Ryan's debut album, *Minor Mutiny*, and contributed two of his compositions to it. Also appearing on the recording is saxophonist Ravi Coltrane, son of John.

TERENCE MICHAEL (TERRY) CLARKE

Born: Vancouver, British Columbia, August 20, 1944

Legends. Once Bill Evans injured his right arm, and played an entire week at New York's Village Vanguard using his left hand only. Pianists filled the place. Once Buddy Rich broke an arm, and played with one hand only. Drummers flocked to see it. Once Shelly Manne broke a leg and played with one foot only. Drummers were amazed. Terry Clarke is part of this odd little fraternity. After breaking an arm in the early eighties, he toured with Jim Hall, playing with one hand, prompting another drummer to voice the opinion that if he broke the other arm, he'd sound twice as good.

Terry came up through the Vancouver jazz world, then slipped down the Pacific coast with bassist and fellow British Columbian Don Thompson to join the John Handy Quintet in San Francisco, a group whose personnel for a short time included fellow Canadian Sonny Greenwich. Then Terry spent two and a half years with the Fifth Dimension at the vocal group's peak of popularity.

Settling in Toronto in the seventies, Terry established himself as a jazz drummer of formidable technique, infallible taste, and enormous range — from Dixieland to the avant-garde, from small groups to big bands. He was a central figure in the Boss Brass and a successful fixture of the studios. In the mid-1980s Terry gradually detached himself from Toronto, setting up permanent residence in New York City. He is a regular member of the Jim Hall Quartet, plays with the Toshiko Akiyoshi Jazz Band, tours, and from time to time returns to Toronto to play with Rob McConnell and the Boss Brass.

He lives with his wife Lesley on Roosevelt Island in an apartment with a sweeping view of the East River and the towers of Manhattan, where his playing is in incessant demand.

JOHN ABERCROMBIE

Born: Port Chester, New York, December 16, 1944

John Abercrombie is mostly Scot: his father, born in England, is half Scottish, and his mother one hundred percent Scottish. When John played outside London with Kenny Wheeler and a stranger approached the band, one of the musicians said, "You're an Abercrombie." The man in fact was a cousin of John's. Another cousin, a film actor in Los Angeles, also has the look. The look? Well, John looks as if he should be tossing the caber or playing the bagpipe or both, not turning out some of the most interesting guitar work of his generation in jazz.

There was no particular predilection for music in his family. John was first interested in rock and roll and blues, then got turned on by two high school friends to the music of Dave Brubeck. He became, and remains, an ardent admirer of Paul Desmond. The recordings Desmond made with Jim Hall turned him on to that guitarist, and Jim's records with Bill Evans to that pianist. John simply decided he wanted to be a musician, and enrolled at the Berklee School (now College) of Music in Boston. He stayed four years and graduated in music education, playing with various Boston musicians and organist Johnny "Hammond" Smith. After Berklee, he settled in Lower Manhattan and worked with drummer Chico Hamilton, the Brecker Brothers, and many others. In 1972 Jack DeJohnette asked him to join a group he was forming, and the two have maintained a close relationship ever since.

John uses some effects drawn from rock and roll and blues bands, but he has refined them; his playing has a rich, muscular, inventive beauty. He also uses the mandolin guitar, which he plays with good effect alongside fellow guitar virtuoso Ralph Towner. He is also a prolific recording artist and an accomplished composer, whose works have been recorded by a number of other jazz players.

John still lives in Lower Manhattan, in a spacious converted loft, with his psychotherapist wife.

CLAUDIO RODITI

Born: Rio de Janeiro, Brazil, May 28, 1946

It's hard to say when the influence of jazz got to Brazil, but certainly the best of the American dance-cum-jazz bands, such as that of Tommy Dorsey, were imported to play at Brazilian gambling casinos in the Big Band Era. Claudio Roditi, son of a Catholic mother and a father of Sephardic ancestry, who worked as a coffee buyer, became aware of jazz through an American uncle, who had a big jazz record collection. Claudio was twelve. His father had encouraged him to learn trumpet. By the late 1950s, Claudio and many other young Brazilian musicians were listening to what in the United States was being called West Coast jazz — the music of Bud Shank, Chet Baker, and especially Gerry Mulligan. This, Claudio says, and other Brazilians agree, had a profound effect on the development of bossa nova, a cooled-down samba.

The first jazz record Claudio bought, when he was fourteen, featured two of the major jazz trumpeters, Roy Eldridge and Dizzy Gillespie. Then he heard his first Miles Davis record, and for a long period would listen to no other trumpeter. "I liked the way Miles played — his tone, space, the lyricism, everything about Miles' playing. Later on I started listening to some other people, and then I realized the importance of the whole direction Dizzy set, through Fats Navarro, Clifford Brown, Booker Little, and all those guys. That became my main line of thought. But I still love space."

Claudio went to Vienna to play in a jazz competition, where he met Art Farmer,

who lives there. Art encouraged him. Claudio returned to Brazil, worked for a time in Mexico City, then in 1970 enrolled at the Berklee School (later College) of Music in Boston. He studied for a year and then went to work. His floating, lyrical playing on trumpet and fluegehlhorn is now a fixture of the New York — and international — jazz world.

TOM HARRELL

Born: Urbana, Illinois, June 16, 1946

Tom, who grew up in San Francisco, became known in jazz through his work with Woody Herman, Horace Silver, and Phil Woods, whom he joined in 1983.

He became known almost as much for his behavior as for his playing. He has a way of standing on the bandstand in an almost catatonic stillness, head hung forward, horn dangling from his hand. When it comes time for him to solo, he will shuffle to the microphone, burn the room down, then retreat into that strange motionless silence.

When Tom Harrell was with Phil Woods, Phil got tired of hearing people say, "What's wrong with your trumpeter?" He would tartly reply, "What's wrong with your ears?"

Since Phil is one of Tom's close friends, he is perhaps the best one to explain: "Tommy is a disabled person. He was diagnosed as schizophrenic in 1967 after the first of several nervous breakdowns. He has been taking stelazine, a powerful psychotropic drug, ever since. He has also suffered from a series of collapsed lung incidents and alcoholism. He no longer drinks.

"Schizophenia is a disorder characterized by loss of contact with one's environment, a deterioration in the ability to function in everyday life, and a disintegration of personality.

"The medications that Tommy has to take to control the chemical imbalance that triggers this disorder have side effects that include muscular weakness and his lethargic appearance.

"The disorder is such that Tommy's mind can deal with only one thing at a time, be it answering a question, playing a solo, or something as simple as pouring a glass of water."

Tom is perfectly aware of his own condition, and is quite droll about it. He is well read, gentle, highly perceptive. And he is held in enormous affection and respect by other musicians. Phil's evaluation: "Tom Harrell is the best musician I ever worked with."

Tom's art remains a thing of beauty, his life an act of courage.

ALAN BROADBENT

Born: Auckland, New Zealand, April 23, 1947

Alan Broadbent and I had just had lunch in a little restaurant in Montecito, California, and we were enjoying the early afternoon sun. An eye-catching woman passed us on the street. Alan said, "And you *know* she just loves Bud Powell!"

It was a funny remark. He meant that any woman he ever loved would have to share his admiration for Bud Powell's artistry on the piano. But, he said, he would never marry. He couldn't take enough time away from music to give to a marriage what it required, and this would only be unfair to the woman. I think he and his actress wife Alison were married within a year. I haven't asked, but I assume she digs Bud Powell. And Debussy, and Mahler.

Bud Powell, Lennie Tristano, and Bill Evans were among Alan's idols when he was growing up in his native New Zealand. Alan remembers the first time he heard Bill. The music was coming from a record

store; he burst into tears at its beauty. After studying at the Royal Trinity College of Music in Auckland, he attended the Berklee College of Music in Boston from 1966 to '69, then became pianist and arranger for the Woody Herman band. I first heard him at that time. He was twenty-two. Woody told me to watch out for this kid, saying he was a major talent. And Wood was right, as usual.

Alan is a superbly lyrical talent, whether in his incarnations as arranger, composer, or player. I am very drawn to such artists. They speak to me in voices I crave to hear. They are about gentleness and love and compassion. We need them in a world groaning under the burden of ugly.

"I feel," Alan says, "that jazz is first of all the art of rhythm. I might have a particular musical personality that comes through, but for me it has to emanate from a sense of an inner pulse. Everything I play is improvised, so as long as my melodic line is generated by this pulse, my left hand plays an accompanying role that relies on intuition and experience as the music demands. The apex of this feeling for me is in the improvisations of Charlie Parker. Regardless of influences, he is my abiding inspiration, and it is to him I owe everything."

JOHN MCNEIL

Born: Yreka, California, March 23, 1948

Yreka, pronounced Why-reek-uh, is a tiny town in the mountains up near the Oregon border. John's father ran a grocery store there. When television came to Yreka in the 1950s, John saw Louis Armstrong playing on a show. "I thought that was the neatest thing to do," he remembers. "I'd never seen anyone play a trumpet, except maybe in a parade." His parents got him one. He didn't know how to remove the mouthpiece, so he couldn't put it back in the case, which didn't close anyway. He started to learn music in school, but the teacher moved to Texas after showing him only the fingering for the C major scale. Unfortunately it had a B-flat in it. "I had trouble with that flat seventh," John says in his dry-as-dust self-deprecating manner. "Maybe this was the birth of jazz, you can't tell. After that I taught myself to play the trumpet. I had to teach myself to read too." He joined a regional swing band when he was fifteen, and listened to Miles Davis and Dizzy Gillespie.

John majored in composition at the University of Portland. "The music school burned down." He didn't graduate in composition because he had a fight with the dean. "It didn't work out. I got a degree in trumpet, which is pretty laughable. I went down to graduate school at the University of Miami. I lasted one semester. I just couldn't hang.

"I went back to California, and basically began starving. That worked out pretty well. A friend of mine said, 'It's too bad you don't play saxophone. There's a country and western band that needs an alto player.' I called the guy up, then borrowed a saxophone. I practiced constantly for two weeks, trying to learn a few little things like the fingering and how to get it in tune. I showed up for the gig. I figured at least I'd get paid for a couple of nights. Somehow they didn't seem to mind. They had this regular gig at a dude ranch. I'm playing alto saxophone in a country band at a dude ranch. I thought, Man, I'm alive, but you can't get much lower than this. A friend called and offered me a jazz gig in Kentucky. I said, 'It'll take me five seconds to pack, and I'm there.'

"In 1978 about eight of us auditioned for Horace Silver. He picked me. I was with him for a year and a half. I've been mostly leading my own bands in the last few years. I guess I'm not a very good employee."

You'd never know from this that John has a trace of talent. He is one of the most admired trumpet players of his generation. Anyone who can record a two-trumpet album with Tom Harrell (his close friend) and not get washed away can't be all bad. John is also an adjunct professor at the New England Conservatory, and one of the most popular teachers on the faculty.

MARC COPLAND (COHEN)

Born: Philadelphia, Pennsylvania, May 27, 1948

No one can ever accuse Marc Copland of being afraid of change. Twenty years ago he was one of the hottest young saxophone players in New York. Abruptly, he abandoned his horns and took up piano, teaching himself how to play. Now he is one of the finest pianists in New York. Having established his name as a pianist, he abandoned the name Cohen and became Marc Copland simply to avoid being confused with a pop singer named Marc Cohn.

Marc, Copland that is, majored in music at Columbia University. He played saxophone in the Chico Hamilton Quintet at the same time John Abercrombie was a member. This initiated a long association between John and Marc. With Abercrombie he made an album called *Friends*, which got excellent reviews.

With the development of electronic augmentations of the saxophone's capabilities, particularly the device called the Echoplex, Marc found he was playing harmony on the horn. He says, "I was writing these tunes, completely unplanned. In the middle of the night, out came these melodies and harmonies. They were obviously from a deep place. When I was coming up as a saxophonist, the ideal was to burn out — to play really intense. All of a sudden here was this impressionist lyrical thing going on inside me that I had known nothing about, rearing its head all by itself. It was so strong that it eventually took me all the way over, not so much because I wanted to play piano—although I grew to love it — but because I had to do something with that feeling. I just decided to switch to piano. That was around 1973. I left New York. I went to California for several months, then upstate New York, and I ended up in Washington for eight or ten years."

He returned to New York and set about establishing himself for a second time. Marc has been a member of the James Moody Quartet and the Bob Belden Ensemble for several years. He has worked with drummer Peter Erskine, saxophonist Joe Lovano, and guitarist John Scofield, and has led his own trio.

Marc and his wife, Joan Beth Lund — an attorney and educational consultant — live in the Riverdale section of New York City.

In the end, Marc hasn't totally obviated confusion. After all, there may be people discovering a pianist named Marc Copland and musing that he sounds a lot like another fine pianist named Marc Cohen. Not to be confused with a saxophonist named Marc Cohen who seems to have disappeared . . .

LAURIE FRINK

Born: Pender, Nebraska, August 8, 1951

Laurie is a lead trumpeter. A lead trumpeter has to have great strength and stamina, because he, or in this case she, pulls not only the trumpet section but the whole band. The band's very intonation hangs on the lead trumpeter. There have been female trumpet players in jazz, but Laurie is the first great woman *lead* trumpeter.

Laurie started playing in a school band in the fifth grade. She studied with a teacher named Dennis Schneider at the University of Nebraska. When she came to New York in the early 1970s, she was a classically trained trumpet player. In New York she looked up Jimmy Maxwell, the great lead trumpeter, who had been in the Benny Goodman band with Bill Crow and Phil Woods when they toured the Soviet Union. She asked him to teach her how to play jazz and lead. Jazz phrasing is very different from the classical, and Jimmy, she says, was patient about showing it to her.

"Gerry Mulligan was getting his Concert Jazz Band back together," Laurie recalls. "He called Jimmy to recommend a young player, and Jimmy recommended me. I had never played in a jazz band before. It scared me, because I didn't know what I was doing. But I really wanted to do it and there were some great musicians in the band who helped me. And Gerry was very tolerant." After that she played lead with Benny Goodman, George Russell, Mel Lewis, and others, as well as in the pit orchestra of more than thirty Broadway musicals.

Laurie continued to study, taking lessons from a famous trumpet teacher named Carmine Caruso, as much a psychotherapist as a music instructor, who had a talent for removing musical blockages. Though he was forty-seven years her senior, she fell in love with him and lived with him for fourteen years until his death in 1987. Laurie is now a teacher herself — of the Carmine Caruso method. "I miss him every day," she says.

Despite her acceptance by such people as Mulligan, Laurie doesn't think the discrimination against women musicians has ended. "Not at all," she says. "I have a friend, a trumpet player, who just got turned down for a job by a leader who said, 'I want a man in that chair.' "

Laurie is essentially a jolly person. But on this subject she shakes her head a little sadly, saying, "Music has no gender."

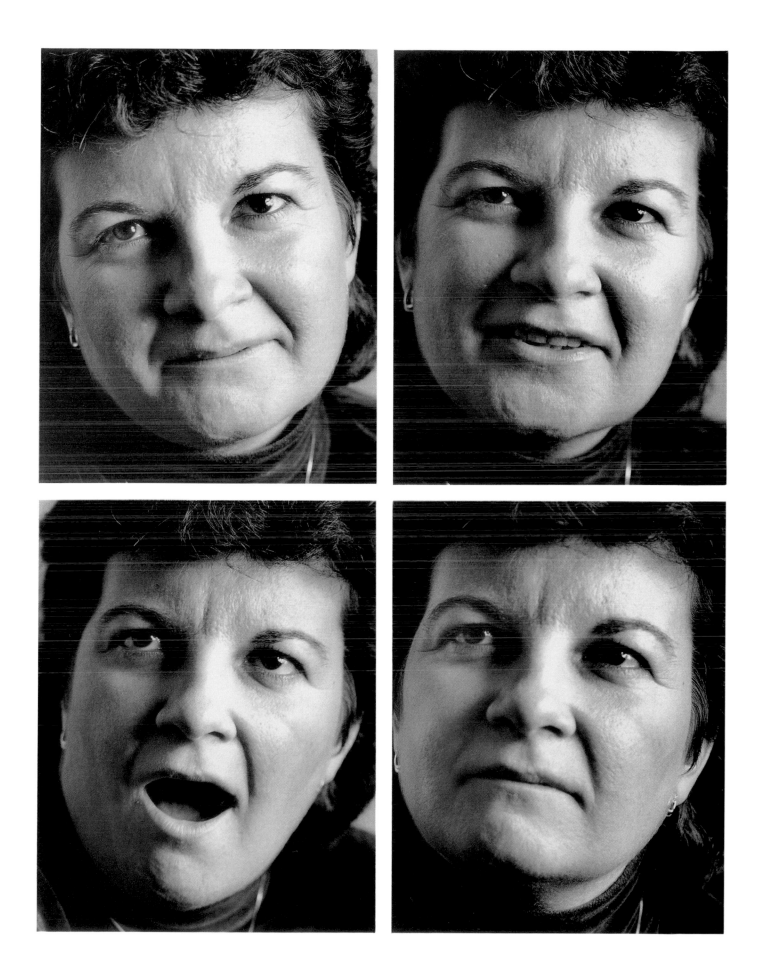

AKIO SASAJIMA

Born: Hakodate, Japan, March 14, 1952

Akio Sasajima is entirely self-taught on guitar. Early in his youth he listened to American movie soundtracks, and then in high school to such pop groups as the Brothers Four, the Kingston Trio, the Ventures, and the Beatles. This is when he began to pick up the instrument. Brazilian music caught his interest, particularly that of guitarist Baden Powell. "And then, right after high school, I heard a Wes Montgomery album," he says. "It knocked me out! I learned to read music on my own, never took a lesson in my life."

He played semi-professionally in Sapporo, the biggest city on the island of Hokkaido, sometimes with visiting saxophonist Sadao Watanabe, who urged him to move to Tokyo. "I was okay, but compared with the professional guys in Tokyo, I was an amateur. It's like New York, you know. After a year I couldn't make a living and I went home for a year. I taught some English." He'd also learned that on his own. (He speaks it just about perfectly, with the slang of a jazz musician.) He began making translations of English music books for a Japanese publisher. Among other projects, he translated a number of the Berklee College of Music textbooks, thereby absorbing their contents.

Akio moved to the United States in 1977, intending to study at Boston's Berklee College of Music, but settled in Chicago, where he soon became active in that city's busy jazz world. "Chicago has tons of good players, though they are not necessarily nationally known," he says. "I played with most of them. Terry Thompson, who is a drummer in Chicago, hired me and I got to play the first Chicago Jazz Festival in 1979."

He has recorded with the Brazilian group Som Brasil, singer Judy Roberts, drummer Victor Lewis, bassist Harvie Swartz, and saxophonist Joe Henderson. He's made two albums with Henderson; the pianist on the second was Renee Rosnes. He also recorded a duet album with the brilliant bassist Ron Carter. In 1991 he returned to Japan on an eighteen-day tour with a group that included Randy Brecker, Don Friedman, Harvie Swartz, and former Miles Davis drummer Jimmy Cobb.

Akio still lives in Chicago, although he is often seen in San Francisco, where he maintains an apartment.

THE CLAYTON BROTHERS
JOHN CLAYTON

Born: Los Angeles, California, August 20, 1952

JEFF CLAYTON

Born: Los Angeles, California, February 16, 1955

When in 1965 Ray Brown was preparing to leave the Oscar Peterson Trio to settle in Los Angeles, Henry Mancini told the bassist to give him a call: Hank said that Ray could do some of his studio work. To Ray's surprise, he went to work for Mancini almost immediately. A few years later Ray gave a workshop in jazz bass at the University of California in Los Angeles. One of the students was a sixteen year old named John Clayton, who until then had studied classical bass. Three years later, Ray recommended John for the television musical series *The Mancini Generation.* Hank hired him on Ray's word. But John told him that he would soon be going off to Indiana University in Bloomington. Hank contracts the rhythm section and a few key players for his national concert tours out of Bloomington. Still never having heard John, he told him, "Call my contractor — you can do my work." All the time he was at Indiana U. (where Bix Beiderbecke once played), John worked for Hank. "If it hadn't been for Mancini, I could have ended up cutting someone's lawn to pay my way through school," he says.

After graduating with a bachelor of music degree, John worked for two years with pianist Monty Alexander, then joined the Count Basie band. For five years, from 1980 through 1984, he was principal bassist with the Amsterdam Philharmonic and lived in Holland.

John and his brother Jeff (w/moustache in photos) come from a family of seven children, raised by their mother, a pianist, organist, and church choir director. Jeff was drawn to the work of alto saxophonist Cannonball Adderley. He studied at California State University at Northridge, majoring in oboe and English horn. "I went to a number of colleges, just so I could play in their bands," he says. He studied privately with respected teacher and saxophonist Bill Green. Jeff plays all the saxophones, all the clarinets and flutes, all the recorders, and, for good measure, harmonica. As one friend said, "He can play anything you can blow."

John and Jeff play together in the Clayton Brothers Quartet and in the nineteen-piece Clayton-Hamilton Jazz Orchestra, formed in 1985 and co-led by John and Jeff Hamilton, John's favorite drummer and friend since their student days at Indiana University.

John divides his time between writing —he made the symphonic arrangement of *The Star-Spangled Banner* for singer Whitney Houston that sold more than a million records in 1991 — and playing. He wants to get into film scoring. He and Jeff Hamilton played on the Natalie Cole *Unforgettable* album. They are a part of a line of brothers who have graced jazz from the beginning, the Dodds, Dorsey, Jones, Heath, Montgomery, Teagarden, McPartland, Swope, and Sims boys, among others, and the twins Art and Addison Farmer.

KEI AKAGI

Born: Sendai, Japan, March 16, 1953

In the mid-twentieth century, the very term *Japanese jazz musician* would have seemed a contradiction in terms. But Japan was exposed to American music after the Second World War, and some of its musicians attempted to play it. At first the results were odd, but gradually they got the hang of it and began to produce good players, including Toshiko Akiyoshi, Sadao Watanabe, and Tiger Okoshi. Pianist Kei Akagi is a brilliant one.

The first time I talked to him and noted his impeccable English, I asked, "How come if you were born in Japan, you talk as if you'd grown up in Cleveland?" It was a shot in the dark; I might just have mentioned St. Louis or any city in the midwest. He said, "Because I grew up in Cleveland." Indeed, he lived from the time he was five in a black neighborhood of that city while his father worked on his Ph.D. in New Testament theology. The family was highly musical. He heard a great deal of Bach and Beethoven in the home, and rhythm and blues in the neighborhood. He started piano lessons at the age of five at the Cleveland Music School Settlement.

The family returned to Japan, where his father became a United Church of Christ minister, when Kei was twelve. Kei studied composition and philosophy at the International Christian University in Tokyo, then was accepted for doctoral studies in philosophy at the University of California at Santa Barbara, where he began composing and arranging for the university's jazz band. He was on his way to being a professor of philosophy, but his musical gifts simply couldn't be ignored. The Brazilian singer Flora Purim and her husband, percussionist Airto Moreira, also lived in Santa Barbara and inevitably heard him. From 1979 to 1985 he was pianist in their group. Then came work with saxophonist Joe Farrell, flutist James Newton, the French jazz violinist Jean-Luc Ponty, guitarist Al DiMeola, and, from 1989 to 1991, Miles Davis, an association that ended six months before Miles died. After that, Kei joined tenor saxophonist Stanley Turrentine. Kei now lives in Los Angeles, busy as a soloist, leader of his own group, composer, arranger, and studio musician.

RICHARD (DICK) OATTS

Born: Des Moines, Iowa, April 2, 1953

Dick's father, an alto player who had played in a navy band in the Second World War and then become a high school band director in Iowa, was his first teacher. Dick majored in flute and minored in piano for a year at Drake University in Des Moines. But it was alto saxophone that became his main instrument. For five years he lived in Minneapolis, where winters were so cold that "you didn't take your clarinet out of the house until the car was warmed up. If you did, the wood would crack in a minute." Dick spent a year on the road with what he described as "a blue-eyed soul band." In 1977 he moved to New York.

He'd been recommended by a mutual friend to arranger and trumpeter Thad Jones, the brilliant brother of Hank and Elvin Jones, who was at that time co-director and chief arranger of the famous Thad Jones-Mel Lewis big band, one of the great training grounds for young musicians. He called Thad from the airport. Thad told him to come immediately to the Village Vanguard to substitute for an alto player who couldn't be there.

Dick entered the Vanguard kitchen, carrying his saxophone case.

"Mel said, 'What are you doing with that?' I said, 'I'm gonna play tonight.' I didn't even know who I was talking to. He said, 'You're gonna *what*?' I said, 'Thad said it would be okay if I played tonight.' He said, 'Thad did *what*?' And he said, 'Can you read music? Can you play the clarinet? Can you play solo, can you play jazz?' I said, 'Yeah, I think so.' He said, 'Whaddya mean, you think so?'

"Thad showed up and said, 'Mel, cool out a little, give this guy a break.'

"It was my first night in New York, and I was playing with my dream band! Of all the big bands that I never thought I'd get on!"

He passed this trial by fire and became one of Mel's favorites. Though he played and recorded with other groups, including Red Rodney's, Dick would stay more than fifteen years with the band, which lives on, though Thad and Mel are gone.

A fellow saxophonist says: "Dick is the best alto player in the business under the age of forty."

WILLIAM JOSEPH (BILL) KIRCHNER, JR.

Born: Youngstown, Ohio, August 31, 1953

"My mother," Bill says, "plays three tunes by ear on piano, including 'Intermission Riff.' The first jazz I can remember hearing included the Henry Mancini scores for *Peter Gunn* and *Mr. Lucky*, which came out when I was about five years old. I started playing clarinet when I was seven because I knew who Benny Goodman was. In 1965, George Wein produced a three-day festival in Pittsburgh. For my twelfth birthday, I talked my parents into taking me. The bill that night was Carmen McRae, Earl Hines with a trio, the Stan Getz Quartet with Gary Burton, Coltrane's quartet with McCoy Tyner, Jimmy Garrison, and Elvin Jones, and the Ellington band. That pushed me over the edge."

Bill studied woodwinds and arranging. He moved to New York to attend Manhattan College, a liberal arts and engineering school, as an English major. But he studied saxophone privately with Lee Konitz from 1971 to '73 and piano with Harold Danko from 1973 to '75. He married his high school sweetheart (they were divorced in 1979), figured he had to get a "real job," and was hired as a writer-editor by the Department of Agriculture in Washington, D.C. While holding down this day job, Bill played with Mike Crotty's big band. Lee Konitz recorded a nonet arrangement Bill wrote on a Wayne Shorter tune.

In 1979 and '80, he studied arranging with Rayburn Wright, head of the jazz studies and contemporary media department at the Eastman School of Music in Rochester, on a National Endowment for the Arts fellowship. "He influenced a lot of good writers," Bill says.

Bill moved back to New York in 1980. "I'm still studying," Bill said. "I've been studying with John McNeil for the last three years, a lot of harmonic things, concepts of improvising and sculpting solos."

Bill has played for the American Jazz Orchestra, Anita O'Day, Mel Lewis, Mousey Alexander, Bobby Rosengarden, Vince Giordano, and his own nonet, and written for people as disparate as Dizzy Gillespie and singer Patti Austin. Though he is a fine saxophonist, clarinetist, and flutist, his growing reputation is as a composer and arranger.

Despite the German name, Bill is Italian on his mother's side and mostly Scottish and Irish on his father's. Bill is potentially a great critic. He is observant and appreciative of the work of others, encyclopedic in his knowledge, and a very good writer. Indeed, he has written reviews and articles for the Washington *Post*. He refuses to write criticism, however, feeling that it would compromise his position as a musician.

One day in late 1991, Bill got a letter of admiration for his nonet recordings from another composer who had used that instrumentation. It was signed: Gerry Mulligan.

JANE IRA BLOOM

Born: Newton, Massachusetts, January 12, 1955

A good many saxophonists have played soprano as a second instrument. Jane Ira Bloom specializes in it. The instrument has a tendency to a greenish kind of oboe sound. Jane gets an enormous, round, warm vocal sound from it. How? "It probably has a lot to do with Joe Viola, my teacher in Boston," she said. "And it has to do with spending a lot of time with the soprano as an instrument in its own right. And trying to get a sound on it that *you* want. Not what the instrument wants! It's an instrument that you have to finesse, there's no doubt about it. It's a rather difficult one. It takes a bit of time to be able to sing through the instrument, sing with *your* voice. It takes a little bit of application. A lot."

Her father was a camp counselor. Her mother had a broad record collection. Jane started saxophone at a very early age. She studied composition at the Yale University school of music, where she met her future husband, Joe Grifasi, a drama student working in the Yale Repertory Company. She stayed there five years, getting a bachelor's and then master's degree in music, then moving to New York in 1976.

She speaks constantly of singing on an instrument, and seems to view all instruments as vocal: "I suppose that the people in the jazz tradition can be credited with trying to get their own voices through the saxophone. That's what you're hearing, their unique and individual voices coming through their instruments: Coleman Hawkins, Sonny Rollins, all the greats. I think that's what's in the honesty of the music."

Jane is a highly original and very lyrical player. She is increasingly recognized as a composer. She was the first composer ever commissioned by NASA to write a piece for its documentary art program. This work, for fifty-piece orchestra, was performed at the Cape Kennedy Space Center in 1989 and again at Carnegie Hall in 1990.

The huge sound Jane gets on soprano seems at variance with her build, which is delicate. Her speech is diffident and gentle. Jane and her husband live in a sunny apartment on the West Side of New York, from where he commutes to Los Angeles for work in films and television.

BRIAN LYNCH

Born: Milwaukee, Wisconsin, September 12, 1956

The graduates of the Art Blakey and Horace Silver groups would fill a substantial hall. Brian Lynch is an alumnus of both groups. He was born a year after Charlie Parker died and grew up in the era of the *Bitches Brew* album by Miles Davis, the late recordings of John Coltrane, and jazz-rock fusion. Brian said: "I think in common with a lot of musicians my age, I went through the music's evolution backwards. I listened to the Art Ensemble of Chicago, stuff like that. I was enamored of the avant-garde. I had to go back. Even to get to Bird was going a little far back for me. Then Art Tatum, Roy Eldridge — I had a lot of catching up to do. Still do."

Brian's father is a counseling psychologist, his mother a teacher. He started learning trumpet in public school, then attended the Wisconsin Conservatory of Music and worked in local groups, including that of pianist and vibraharpist Buddy Montgomery, Wes Montgomery's brother. He worked for a short period with Charles McPherson in San Diego, California, after paying a number of visits to New York, where he met Claudio Roditi, who encouraged him. After he moved to New York in 1981, Claudio got him some of his first jobs. Brian's affinity for Latin music found him work with a number of Brazilian, Puerto Rican, and Cuban groups. He was with the Horace Silver Quintet from October 1982 until 1985. "Horace showed me a lot about consistency in playing," Brian says. "He set a very high standard." For two years, from December 1988 until October 1990, he was with Art Blakey and the Jazz Messengers; he was thus the last trumpeter to play with Blakey. "This was the greatest experience in my career so far," he recalls. "Art taught me so much as a musician and as a man." Brian also played with Jack McDuff and the Toshiko Akiyoshi big band, and for eight years in Bill Kirchner's nonet. He went to Europe in 1989 with Benny Golson and Art Farmer in a group that also included Jackie McLean and Curtis Fuller.

In March 1992, Brian became a member of the Phil Woods Quintet, replacing the gifted trombonist Hal Crook, who in turn had replaced Tom Harrell.

GERI ALLEN

Born: Pontiac, Michigan, June 12, 1957

Geri was born in the same town as Elvin and Thad Jones. Geri started studying piano at the age of seven. When she said she grew up in Detroit, I asked immediately, "Cass Tech?"

"How did you know?" she said. Because of course so many of that city's best jazz musicians, including Donald Byrd, Barry Harris, and the late Frank Rosolino, came out of that school.

"I was in a madrigal group led by one of Donald Byrd's contemporaries, Marilyn Jones," Geri said. "She also had the jazz ensemble. I'll never forget that she got him to come there, and he raised money for us to go to Australia. That was my first trip out of the country. It was an award-winning group, and from his sharing himself, we got to make that trip. And then he inspired everybody, just by talking with us about what was going on and what was necessary to making it out there."

From Cass Tech, she went on to study piano with John Malachy at Howard University, getting her bachelor's degree in 1979, and did graduate studies in musicology at the University of Pittsburgh. "While I was in school," she said, "I was unhappy about it, but in retrospect I'm glad. My parents pushed me. My father is a retired educator, who taught in the public-school system in Detroit for thirty-five years. My grandmother taught in a one-room school house. Most of my aunts and uncles are in education. I had to do it." She moved to New York in 1982, and has built a solid professional reputation that is still growing.

Geri's manner is gentle and soft. Her husband is a jewelry designer. The day John Reeves and I visited, her baby daughter, just recovering from a cold, was sleeping in a playpen next to Geri's grand piano. Motherhood makes travel impractical for the present, but she did manage for a time to commute one day a week to Boston to teach at the New England Conservatory of Music.

"In my generation," Geri said, "I think the roots of the music have a very strong hold. I see that more than I don't see it — people who take the time to look at the tradition. A lot of the pianists of my generation are playing Fats Waller and looking at the beginnings."

No one, but no one, applies to Geri Allen the bromide "She plays good for a girl." Geri is at the forefront of the avant-garde in jazz piano, at home playing with Paul Motian and Charlie Haden and with Young Turks such as saxophonist Steve Coleman.

CHRISTIAN JACOB

Born: Metz, France, May 8, 1958

Christian Jacob started studying piano at the age of four and a half. His father, a jeweler who played piano part-time, gave Christian a book of old songs, including some of George Gershwin's. Christian was immediately fascinated by the harmony.

He won first prize in piano performance at the Conservatoire National de Région in his native Metz in 1970, when he was twelve years old. In 1978, at the age of twenty, he took the same prize at the Conservatoire National Superiéur in Paris. "I was always into jazz," Christian says, "and I was playing jazz for recreation, though my teachers at the Conservatory didn't like it and were telling me not to do it. I was interested in it really very early." After graduating from the Conservatoire, he went home to teach piano in his old school in Metz. Then he went to the Berklee College of Music, where he took a degree in professional music *magna cum laude*. He won the Joe Zawinul Jazz Masters Award at Berklee in 1985, and in 1986 the Oscar Peterson Jazz Masters Award. He then joined the staff of the college, teaching piano there from 1986 to 1990.

A fellow student at Berklee was Wilder Ferguson, one of Maynard Ferguson's four daughters. She was studying voice. In 1984 Christian gave her a tape to give to Maynard, who was impressed by it — so much so that he began to use Christian on the road in a quintet. Meanwhile, relations with Wilder Ferguson were growing closer, and in October 1989 she and Christian were married. Soon after that they moved to California where Christian became musical director and arranger for Maynard's Big Bop Nouveau Band.

Christian has also worked with Michael Brecker, Eddie Gomez, Steve Gadd, Peter Erskine, John Abercrombie, and Benny Carter, and toured extensively with Gary Burton, who recorded some of Christian's compositions.

Though he returns to Europe to conduct on his own, Christian finds working for his father-in-law is pretty much a full-time job.

KENNETH (KENNY) WASHINGTON

Born: Brooklyn, New York, May 29, 1958

Benny Golson warned me about Kenny Washington before I met him. "Unless you're prepared to listen for three hours, don't ask him anything about jazz history, especially drums. He'll start probably with Baby Dodds and take you on to Tony Williams and beyond." Benny was right. I asked a question or two, and found that Kenny — aside from being a highly admired drummer in the bebop tradition — is a formidable scholar of the music's history. When John Reeves and I visited him, he was living in a small, sparsely furnished apartment in Brooklyn, surrounded by his huge record collection, whose contents he knows thoroughly.

As in so many cases, it was a parent who fostered the interest in music. Kenny's father, a computer operator for IBM, had a huge and eclectic record collection, to which Kenny was constantly exposed. And his father, "a Duke Ellington and Count Basie freak," took him to see these and other bands.

Growing up in Staten Island, Kenny started playing drums around the age of six. He attended the High School of Music and Arts in Manhattan, and took private lessons as well. Then he went to work for alto saxophonist Lee Konitz, who introduced him to Mel Lewis. Mel, a great drummer and one of the great nurturers in jazz, took him under his wing, teaching him an enormous amount about adaptability to various musical situations, from accompanying a singer, through playing in small groups to playing in a big band. Kenny recalls that Mel's first lesson was this: "You play too loud. And you're not using your bass drum." Once Kenny looked down as he was playing to discover that Mel was under the piano, watching his footwork.

Kenny was about twenty when he met Mel, who promptly asked him, "Are you married? — No? Stay that way." So far Kenny has followed that advice.

Kenny says that he also learned a lot listening to the Oscar Peterson Trio when Ed Thigpen was with it, as well as the Ahmad Jamal and Jo Jones trios. When Mel Lewis was growing weak from cancer, he repeatedly paid Kenny the ultimate compliment: he would send Kenny in as his substitute with Mel's big band. Kenny's memories of Mel are warm, poignant, charming, and funny.

Kenny has recorded with Johnny Griffin, Kenny Burrell, Ron Carter, Frank Wess, Phil Woods, Benny Carter, Betty Carter, Milt Jackson, George Coleman, Cedar Walton, and many others — on a total of more than eighty albums so far. And now he has his own students, who come from around the world.

More recently, he has conducted his own FM radio show in New York, drawing on his own huge record library. No one is more qualified to do it than this eloquent, charming, and gifted young man.

IGOR BUTMAN

Born: Leningrad, Russia, October 27, 1961

OLEG BUTMAN

Born: Leningrad, July 9, 1966

Like Adam Makowicz, the Butman brothers — Igor, tenor saxophone, and Oleg, drums — are children of Willis Conover. Or perhaps grandchildren, since their father, Mikhail Butman, an engineer and amateur drummer, was already a fan of Louis Armstrong and Benny Goodman. Igor's saxophone teacher, Genady Goldstein, told him to listen to the *Music USA* broadcasts. Igor describes how, at Russian jazz concerts, the announcers would affect low, slow voices, imitating Conover "to try to sound cool."

Their father was in the audience when the Benny Goodman band, with Bill Crow and Phil Woods in its personnel, toured the Soviet Union just before Igor's birth. Phil became friends with Genady Goldstein.

Igor (right in photos), who first trained on clarinet, just wanted to play rock and roll guitar. "From the day I met Genady Goldstein," Igor said, "I wanted to play jazz. I forgot about rock and roll the first day I met him."

Then Igor met visiting American musicians, including Grover Washington, Dave Brubeck, Pat Metheny, and Billy Taylor. Billy sat in with Igor's quartet in Moscow. And vibraharpist Gary Burton helped Igor get a full scholarship to the Berklee College of Music, where he enrolled in 1987 and studied for two years. There he met Al Grey's son Michael. "We became very good friends," he said. Grover Washington introduced him to Al Grey himself, and Grey let him sit in with his group.

Oleg started out playing balalaika, but that is hardly a traditional jazz instrument, so Igor, who needed a drummer, urged him to play drums. Oleg followed his brother to the United States, continued to study and grow, and found work with people of the stature of Monty Alexander.

Both brothers say that residence in the United States has changed their playing. "It's changed it a lot, in terms of sound, understanding of time and feel, everything," Igor says. "Just to be able to see some other people playing, very good players. When you see somebody doing something, and you're right there, not listening to a record, you think you can do the same thing, try to play different."

The Butman brothers took an apartment on the West Side in New York. Funny, witty, and charming, immersed now in American music in the land of its origin, they struck me as being like two kids let loose in a toy store.

RENEE ROSNES

Born: Regina, Saskatchewan, March 24, 1962

Adopted when she was four months old, Renee grew up in Vancouver with new parents who loved music. They started her studying piano when she was three and violin when she was five. In high school she became interested in jazz, developing a taste for Miles Davis and John Coltrane. As a pianist, she was particularly influenced by Cedar Walton, Thelonious Monk, Oscar Peterson, and Herbie Hancock. After two years at the University of Toronto, she returned to Vancouver, where she played engagements with Dave Liebman and the late Joe Farrell. She spent two summers at the Banff Centre, where Don Thompson and Kenny Wheeler were teaching.

She moved to New York City in 1986 and joined Joe Henderson's quartet in January 1987. Henderson became her staunch champion, describing her as "lyrical beyond her years." "It's unusual for musicians of her generation to have so much depth," he says. He recorded with her and took her on tour in the United States, Europe, and Japan. In 1988 she toured with saxophonist Wayne Shorter and then with J.J. Johnson. The next year she toured and recorded with trumpeter Jon Faddis. She's worked with Dizzy Gillespie, James Moody, Robin Eubanks, Ralph Moore, and Buster Williams.

Renee is in the forefront of younger pianists. Her playing is at once powerful and deeply lyrical. In ballads it is gorgeous, and at up tempos daring, plunging, and absolutely fearless. She also is emerging as an interesting and very personal composer.

Renee tours frequently and records for Blue Note with a trio of her own. The drummer is Billy Drummond. He is also her husband. They met in a band called Out of the Blue, which also recorded for Blue Note records. "Both of us work with other people as well," she says. "It's not as if we're exclusively together. We do a lot of work together, and we think it's great. We get along very well on stage, musically, and we get along off stage. It's worked out fine." They live in Brooklyn.

THE HARPER BROTHERS
WINARD HARPER

Born: Baltimore, Maryland, June 4, 1962

PHILIP HARPER

Born: Baltimore, Maryland, May 10, 1965

Winard (above right) is the older of the two Harper brothers who, with their group, emerged among the hottest young players of the early 1990s, and he takes the role of leader and manager. He is a perfectionist, with a constant concentration on his craft. Even in conversation while riding in a car, he will be found drumming with a pair of sticks on his knee. Buddy Rich was like that: he would drum his way along the walls of a corridor on the way to the stage.

Younger brother Philip is one of the outstanding trumpet players of his generation. A major influence on them, they will tell you, is an older brother, trumpeter and pianist Danny Harper. Winard was playing drums in Danny's group, in Baltimore and Atlanta, when he was only five. Danny started teaching Philip to play trumpet when Philip was eleven.

Philip says that he and Roy Hargrove have a taste for the same trumpet players, Freddie Hubbard, Clifford Brown, and Lee Morgan. Philip is yet another one of the alumni of Art Blakey; he wishes he had spent even more time with that master drummer and teacher. Winard, like Benny Golson and Shirley Horn, is an alumnus of Howard University.

The brothers moved to New York, then attended the University of Hartford in Connecticut on scholarships to study with saxophonist Jackie McLean. Winard then played with two giants of the tenor saxophone, Dexter Gordon and Johnny Griffin. The brothers returned to New York, where Winard joined singer Betty Carter. Philip played some gigs with organist Jimmy McGriff (who appears on their album *You Can Hide Inside the Music*, along with singer Ernie Andrews).

Like generations of trumpet players before him, Philip faced the fierce competition of New York City. "It's like being the fastest gun in the west," he says. "Everywhere you go there's somebody who wants to take you on."

Winard likes to listen to tapes of the late Jo Jones, and he goes to hear Billy Higgins play. "Those guys," he said once, "sat behind the drums like it was Christmas morning. That's the way I want to play my music, like a little kid on Christmas morning."

ROY HARGROVE

Born: Waco, Texas, October 16, 1969

Roy Hargrove started playing trumpet in a Dallas elementary school band, then went on to that city's Arts Magnet High School, whose band director introduced him to the recordings of Clifford Brown. "I haven't really been the same since," Hargrove told Jon Pareles of the *New York Times*. "I found it hard to believe a trumpet player like that, because he had covered so much of the horn technically, but the sound was so warm and brassy. Then the next trumpet player I heard was Freddie Hubbard, and that really turned my head around."

From the time he started listening to the great masters, Roy lived and breathed music. Wynton Marsalis heard Roy when he was seventeen, and became his champion. Roy went on to the Berklee College of Music in Boston for a year and a half, but by then he was already performing professionally in New York, his playing acquiring increasing polish and maturity. Meanwhile, he studied part-time under Donald Byrd at the New School for Social Research.

He quickly found himself playing in the company of such people as Frank Morgan and Carmen McRae. Larry Clothier, Carmen's manager, soon took over the direction of Hargrove's career, placing him with more seasoned players and sending him on a tour of Europe. Early in 1990 Roy signed his first recording contract, and in April 1991 he performed as a special guest in a Carnegie Hall concert with Sonny Rollins, one of his heroes.

"I was nervous, man," Roy said later.

"He's very powerful onstage. If you're not ready, you'll look like a little kid up there. They expected me to be intimidated, but I wasn't."

No indeed. One of the characteristics of his playing is its assurance. That, and lyricism, and a wonderful command of the instrument.

Since 1990, he has been leading his own quintet, featuring another of the talented youngbloods, saxophonist Antonio Hart, who had been a schoolmate at Berklee.

GEOFF KEEZER

Born: Au Claire, Wisconsin, November 20, 1970

The first person who told me about Geoff Keezer was Benny Golson. The second was Art Farmer. When rumor gets that strong, it's time to pay attention.

Geoff was the last pianist to play in the quintet of Art Blakey, that incomparable discoverer, nurturer, and mentor of young talent. Geoff was eighteen when he joined Blakey, filling a chair once occupied by another great nurturer, Horace Silver. That was a year after John Reeves and I began work on this book. I never got a chance to hear Geoff with that group. I didn't hear him until Art Farmer asked me in the spring of 1992 to write liner notes for an album he'd recorded in Japan with Geoff on piano. I was overwhelmed by the prowess, power, and imagination of Keezer's work, which already had its own stamp and identity—not to mention a huge blazing technique.

Both Geoff's parents are musicians. His father, a drummer, teaches music at the University of Wisconsin at Au Claire. His mother, a French horn player, teaches music in junior high school in Au Claire. Thus when I asked Geoff when his musical training started, I was not surprised by the answer: "About the day I was born." His mother was his first teacher, but then he had a succession of classical teachers— in other words, the conventional training for jazz pianists. Then he studied for a year at the Berklee College of Music in Boston. His discoverer was James Williams, himself an outstanding pianist, who recommended him to Blakey.

"I met a lot of people with Art," Geoff

said. "All of my heroes had played with him at one time or another, and they would come by to see him. That's how I met Art Farmer."

At the time of this writing, Geoff works with Art Farmer, Benny Golson, and tenor saxophonist George Coleman when they call on him. He has already formed a quartet and recorded two albums on his own. A year ago I'd never heard of him. We're going to be hearing about him for years and years to come. *Vive la jeunesse.*

CHRISTOPHER (CHRIS) POTTER

Born: Columbia, South Carolina, January 1, 1971

In 1987, when I was visiting Columbia, South Carolina, friends urged me to go to a club to hear a sixteen-year-old saxophonist named Chris Potter. His mother, I was told, was a professor of child psychology at the University of South Carolina and his father, who had done chromosome research at the University of Chicago, now worked for the South Carolina Department of Education. I was astonished at the strength and comparative maturity of the boy's playing.

Four years later in New York, that boy, now a precocious twenty, told me: "I was into rock and roll in fourth or fifth grade. For some reason I was interested in the saxophone. That led me into pursuing the style called jazz. I remember the first thing I heard was Paul Desmond and Dave Brubeck, *Take Five*. I think I'd always heard the saxophone in a rock and roll context, that harsh, ugly sound. And then I heard Paul Desmond make it really pretty.

"I started studying the summer before fifth grade. I started with alto. I was really into Johnny Hodges with Ellington. Most of the young guys I talk to get into it from today first, and then learn the history later.

"I studied with guys in Columbia, and professors in the jazz department at the university helped me a lot. I played in the U.S.C. big band under Roger Pemberton all through middle school and high school.

"And I came to New York when I was eighteen."

Not without trepidation on his mother's part, to be sure. She urged him to stay out of the subway. "But my folks have really been supportive," Chris said. "They know this is what I really want to do, and that it's pretty crazy to want to do it.

"Jazz is not something you go into expecting to make any money. I just enjoy doing it, and I feel that whatever contribution I'm going to make in the world, it's going to be from music. To do anything else would not be right, at least for me."

Two months after he arrived in New York, Chris replaced Dick Oatts in the Red Rodney Quintet, and played on an album called *Red Alert*. A brilliant career obviously lies ahead.

CHRISTIAN MCBRIDE

Born: Philadelphia, Pennsylvania, May 31, 1972

As with Geoff Keezer, Benny Golson was the first person to pull my coat to his very young fellow Philadelphian, Christian McBride. I knew that Chris should be in this book. "But," I said to Benny, "I *know* what to talk to you about. About the old days, about everything back to when you and Coltrane were kids getting started. But what do you ask someone who's nineteen?"

Benny laughed and said, "Ask him where he was last week."

John Reeves and I found Chris, a young man with a wonderful smile and a shy kind of laugh, in a funky little apartment in Brooklyn. I reminded myself that Gerry Mulligan had written "Disc Jockey Jump" for Gene Krupa when Gerry was Chris McBride's age, and that Zoot Sims and Stan Getz were not out of their teens when they joined Woody Herman, who himself had led his first band when he was twenty-two. Still, Chris McBride seemed awfully young.

Chris wanted to emulate his father, who plays electric bass. His mother bought him his own electric bass when he was eight. An uncle who plays stand-up acoustic bass got him interested in jazz when he was eleven. Chris studied bass from the seventh grade on, attended Philadelphia's High School for Creative and Performing Arts, then went to Juilliard for a year. He soon was receiving so many calls to work that he had to quit school. He told us:

"I take lessons when I can with my old bass teacher at Juilliard, Homer Mensch, who is retired from the New York Philhar-

monic. He started with them in the 1930s. "I started to work professionally in Philadelphia when I was thirteen. I met Benny Golson in 1986. He was doing a radio show in Philly, and I was hanging out at the studio. Of course I knew who he was. I was just sitting there listening to the interview he was giving. I just kind of went up and talked to him. Four years later, he called me up. I still hadn't met him formally since then. He left a message, saying: 'I've been hearing a lot of great things about you and I'd like you to go to Europe with me.' I said, 'Oh man!' So we left together, Benny, Curtis Fuller, Tony Reams, Geoff Keezer, and Brian Lynch."

John took this portrait of nineteen-year-old Chris in February 1991, in his Brooklyn apartment. One year later, he was one of the most sought-after bass players in New York, and had moved into Manhattan and an apartment on Lexington Avenue. His history lies mostly before him. If he enjoys the constitution of Spiegle Willcox and Benny Carter, he will probably be playing jazz beyond the year 2050.

Afterword

Jazz Lives

Almost from its earliest days, some of the admirers of jazz have been announcing its imminent demise. Each advance in the music has been denounced as a virus that would destroy it, the prognosis being issued with indignant ferocity. I know of no art that has inspired such partisan division.

When Louis Armstrong departed from the practices of New Orleans polyphony, admirers of that music lamented the sacrilege. After Armstrong came 1930s small group swing and the big band jazz explosion. This "modernism" was considered treasonous. Then in the 1940s came bebop: the schism it caused was bitter. Bebop was called "Chinese music" by the one faction, who in turn were abused as moldy figs by the advocates of bop.

And the cry "Bebop killed the big bands!" was heard in the land, although it was patently absurd: not all the bands took up the new music and the public was perfectly free to patronize those that did not and to ignore bebop if it preferred a harmonically and rhythmically simpler music. Some fundamentalists were still clinging to this tenet forty years after bebop arrived, ignoring the historical fact that it was just those bands that accepted and accommodated elements of it that survived, including those of Woody Herman and Count Basie. Duke Ellington had no trouble absorbing players with bebop proclivities, such as Clark Terry, into his own overall style. Later on, Ellington recorded with John Coltrane. Ellington survived as a bandleader into the 1970s, Basie and Herman into the eighties, and all three bands are still extant under other leaders. They may play on in the dawn of the twenty-first century; their music has become part of the living repertoire as surely as that of Mozart, Johann Strauss, and Debussy. Bebop didn't kill the big bands, various social forces did the job.

If successive groups of people wanted whatever form of jazz they favored to remain fixed forever, another group has continually peered, hand shading forehead, into the future, asking a question which became anathema to jazz musicians: "Where is jazz going?" Legend has it that Stan Kenton once replied, "Well, we're going to Kansas City."

Back in 1934, in a book entitled *Music Ho!*, the British conductor, composer, and writer Constant Lambert examined what had happened to European concert music. It seemed to have advanced as far as it could go, he thought, certainly as far as the audience could follow, and some composers were resorting to what he called "time traveling," moving back and forth in historical periods. Jazz critics would lay the same charge on alto saxophonist Julian (Cannonball) Adderley, among others, and started using terms such as "neo-conservatism," "neo-bop," "bebop revival movement."

When jazz began to be taken seriously as art, many of its chroniclers and commentators, it seems to me, looked to classical-music critics for their models, and in the process made a fundamental mistake. Classical music is largely a *written* tradition. Jazz is an oral tradition, based on the precedents of other players, the study of their records, and, when possible, the absorption of personal lessons from those who, like Dizzy Gillespie, Phil Woods, Clark Terry, and more, were willing to pass their knowledge along in clinics or just private conversation. In that sense, I suppose, you can make a somewhat tenuous claim that jazz is a folk art. But then so is the use of personal computers, since the manuals are incomprehensible and we teach each other to use the equipment. Though jazz is now taught in thousands of schools, its tradition still is primarily communicated through listening to records and emulating its masters. Thus it is not only an oral tradition, it is an aural one. Though most jazz musicians read music well, jazz is not about reading, it is about playing, and above all about improvising in (as Jane Ira Bloom emphasizes) a personal voice.

When jazz became respectable — and legend to the contrary, many American intellectuals proclaimed its importance from its early days — a number of writers arose to argue its case. Few among them had any real technical or historical background in music — which is strange, in that the musicians usually have a considerable knowledge of classical music, as indeed do many members of the lay jazz audience. These critics were mostly fans with typewriters; one of them was an electrical engineer. I have often thought that one of the most unfortunate things that happened to jazz was to be proclaimed an art form, for that made it self-conscious and some of it became pretentious. But worst of all, those eager writers who cried out for its respectability adopted the model of classical-music criticism. And classical-music criticism was itself fundamentally flawed, since it looked on music as exploration rather than expression. That is to say, to be considered important, the composer was expected to revise and "expand" the musical language, not merely use it. If he did not do so, he was not "original."

This view, which developed in the nineteenth century, was, I think, the misapplication to art of the experience of science. Why, you could see it for yourself. In the branches of science, new discoveries constantly caused the revision or superannuation of previous models of reality. New "truths" replaced old and then in turn were themselves superseded, which of course they could not have been if they had ever been truths in the first place. The scientists of our own time have at last attained what may be the one sensible scientific truth: that we cannot know reality, we can only design models of it, subject to revision as we get more "information."

The nineteenth century began with Beethoven, a young piano virtuoso of thirty-one. Mozart had been considered the finest improviser of his age, and according to contemporary accounts, Beethoven surpassed him. In 1800 he gave a concert in which his First Symphony was performed. After that the vocabulary of music expands rapidly, with Beethoven's late quartets sometimes seeming to anticipate jazz in their harmonic usage and coloration. It was inevitable that music would seem to be "progressing." So it was in science; so it must also be in art.

But, matters of formal structure aside, the "progress" consisted to a large extent of exploring harmony. By the time of Arnold Schoenberg's maturity, the methodology seemed to have become so complicated that he rejected it and developed a system of twelve-tone or serial composition, in effect declaring all tones equal, none being more important than the other, and he created a kind of music that almost a century later remains bafflingly impenetrable to the layman.

The idea that art is an unending exercise in revolution is a doubtful one even for classical music, and it is utterly inapplicable to jazz, if only because jazz is primarily an oral rather than a written tradition. There is one other way in which it differs, perhaps even more important. We have noted that the master composers in and before Beethoven's time were also master performers and improvisers. As the nineteenth century pro-

204

gressed, music became a matter of master composers and their minions, the orchestra players who lived only to reproduce the music of other men. A great division opened between the creation of music and its re-creation. A performer was judged by how well he played someone else's work, a standard that in classical music still prevails. But jazz restored the oneness of creation and performance, the tradition of masterful improvisation. And it expanded the art in that it developed a system of group improvisation. It thereby created a perfect paradigm of democracy, with the voice and message and emotions of each participant held in due respect. This doubtless is one of the reasons dictators in recent decades have hated and proscribed it. It is also a reason, we might note in passing, that musicians living under tyrannies like that of (until recently) Poland or even highly structured societies like that of Japan — for example, Adam Makowicz and Kei Akagi, respectively — should have perceived in jazz an escape into freedom.

What jazz did in the first half of its life was to follow the pattern of European harmonic evolution, exploring the implications of the overtone series. But there are evident limits to what an audience can hear. And it was all too easily forgotten that serialism had not found much of a following a half century after its development; it still hasn't, after the better part of a century. Much twentieth-century classical music has been interesting primarily to a small group of specialists. For the most part it has survived in a greenhouse atmosphere of grants, endowments, and patronage, sequestered from the withering winds of reality.

Jazz has enjoyed no such indulgence. While it is true that the music has been admired and praised by leading intellectuals and thoughtful musicians since its early days, it is also true that some of the members of the cultural establishment have been frightened by its energy, immediacy, and emotion. Now, to be sure, thousands of courses on playing jazz are taught throughout North America, but there has been no such expansion of courses in its appreciation, comparable to, say, English literature courses. The jazz musician still must attract an audience. And it is, I think, out of the tension of serving two masters, the artist's own inner sense of what is the best and highest in his work on the one hand and the limitations of a lay though willing audience on the other, that jazz has kept its head when all the musics about it were losing theirs, whether the coarsest and most ignorant of current pop music or the most arcane and uncompromising of intellectualized "classical" music.

Jazz is best appreciated by those who couple a measure of intellectual understanding with a desire and capacity to feel. This is its greatness. It is to me the music that speaks best to and for our time, this remarkable art that began to formulate itself in the Louisiana delta as the century began and by century's end has become first a special and highly intelligent musical language for America and finally an idiom for all the world.

I pay no attention to those who coin terms like "neo-traditionalist" and "bebop revivalist." The jazz composer-player — for in jazz the two have again become one — can and does borrow on the whole rich tradition of this music in a way that the classical composer is enjoined from doing.

I am reminded of a comment by John Clayton, who has had success in both the classical and jazz worlds: "The influences in jazz are enormous. The things that we have to draw from, I think, are what makes it so expansive, especially when you compare it to classical music. In classical music there are more rules that allow you to accept or reject the music. If you don't play Mozart and composers of that period in that style, then it's quote 'wrong.' In jazz we invite your contributions to stride or bebop or whatever it is. If you want to throw some different stuff in there, it's welcome. It's wanted, in fact."

This is a difference of great magnitude.

Jazz is not "going" anywhere. It is there. It has explored and consolidated its conventions and vocabulary. If you consider the work of only the pianists in this book — Oscar Peterson, Cedar Walton, Horace Silver, McCoy Tyner, Roger Kellaway, Warren Bernhardt, Lou Levy, Alan Broadbent, Geri Allen, Renee Rosnes among them — you will realize that they achieve highly personal and deeply moving music out of the same vocabulary on the same instrument. This is a far greater creativity, to my mind, than a constant anxious search for originality through altering the vocabulary of the art. In the sense of the artist's improvising original expression out of known vocabulary and a strong tradition, jazz has gone back to Bach.

If our species survives, and as an American folk expression has it, "the Good Lord willing and the creek don't rise," Roy Hargrove and Chris Potter will be making jazz fifty years from now, and Renee Rosnes and Geri Allen will be something like Myra Hess and Nadia Boulanger when the twenty-first century is fifty years old.

With Spiegle Willcox and Benny Carter still out there and young Kenny Washington, bebop revivalist or not, studying and assimilating the music's tradition, it is ludicrous for anyone to say that jazz is dying.

Quite to the contrary. Jazz lives.

Gene Lees

Selected Recordings

This list of recordings, arranged alphabetically by the artist's last name, is based in part on apparent availability. Jazz records are listed in Spectrum, the new name of the Schwann catalogue, and in Phonolog, a loose-leaf book kept by most record stores. Neither is complete. This list is by no means definitive, nor does it necessarily represent the "best" of each musician. It does, however, include what might be called representative work.

Jazz records do not receive good distribution. The reader is recommended to obtain the catalogue of Mosaic Records. You can write to the company at 35 Melrose Place, Stamford CT 06902, U.S.A. Mosaic does superb reissues of jazz records, with extensive and informative annotation. Mosaic has a second company, True Blue, which distributes all the Blue Note Records and some Fantasy and Polygram records as well.

Another good mail order source is Cadence, whose address is Cadence Building, Redwood NY 13679, U.S.A. Cadence is both a mail order house and a music publication that each month updates its listings. It has a huge inventory, and provides a service to buyers that is quick and reliable. The personnel are refreshingly courteous.

Most of the albums listed are available on CD.

JOHN ABERCROMBIE: *Characters* (solo); *Gateway* (with Jack DeJohnette); *Getting There*. With Ralph Towner: *Sargasso Sea*, all on ECM.

KEI AKAGI: With Flora Purim and Airto Moreira: *The Magicians*, Concord. With Rufus Reid and Akira Tana: *AAJI, Sound Circle*, King. With Miles Davis: (concert video) *Miles in Paris*, WEA Music Video; *Playroom*, Moo/Blueroom.

GERI ALLEN: With Paul Motian and Charlie Haden: *In the Year of the Dragon*, Jazz Music Today. *In the Middle*, Minor Music; *Open On All Sides*, Minor Music; *The Nurturer*, Blue Note.

ERNIE ANDREWS: *Travelin' Light*, GNP Crescendo. With The Harper Brothers: *You Can Hide Inside the Music*, Verve.

GUIDO BASSO: *Guido Basso* (with Terry Clarke), Innovation. With the Boss Brass: *The Jazz Album*, Attic; *The Brass Is Back*, Concord.

TONY BENNETT: *Jazz*, Sony/CBS; *The Tony Bennett-Bill Evans Album*, Fantasy; *The Movie Song Album*, Columbia.

WARREN BERNHARDT: *Ain't Life Grand; Heat of the Moment; Hands On; Reflections*, all on DMP.

ED BICKERT: *Dance to the Lady* (with Don Thompson), Sackville; *This Is New* (with Lorne Lofsky) Concord; *I Wished on the Moon* (with Rick Wilkins and Terry Clarke), Concord. He is also heard on the Paul Desmond albums recorded at Bourbon Street in Toronto on CTI/CBS.

JANE IRA BLOOM: *Mighty Lights* (with Charlie Haden), Enja; *Modern Drama*; *Slalom*, both CBS.

ALAN BROADBENT: *Another Time*, Trend; *Everything I Love*, Discovery; *Live at Maybeck Recital Hall*, Concord.

BOB BROOKMEYER: *Back Again with Thad Jones and Mel Lewis*, Gazell; *The Dual Role of Bob Brookmeyer*, Fantasy/OJC; *Oslo* (with Alan Broadbent), Concord. Some of Brookmeyer's finest writing is heard on *Gerry Mulligan and the Concert Jazz Band*, Verve.

RAY BROWN: Ray is heard on scores of Oscar Peterson recordings from 1949 through to the present, and as leader on *Live at Concord Jazz*, Concord; *Don't Forget the Blues* (with Al Grey), Concord; *Ray Brown 3*, Concord.

DAVE BRUBECK: *Jazz Goes to College*, Columbia Jazz Masterpieces; *The Essence of Dave Brubeck*, Columbia/Legacy; *Take Five*, Sony/CBS; *Time Out*, Columbia.

IGOR BUTMAN: *Jazznost*, MHS.

OLEG BUTMAN: No recordings.

DONALD BYRD: *At the Half Note*; *Byrd in Hand*; *Fuego*; *I'm Trying to Get Home*, all on Blue Note; *Harlem Blues*, Landmark.

PETE AND CONTE CANDOLI: Though both men have recorded extensively as side men, the Candolis are sparsely represented as leaders. Some of Pete's best early work is with Woody Herman's First Herd, whose recordings are periodically re-released by CBS. One of these is the CD *The Thundering Herds 1945-47*. Conte is heard to advantage on many of the Supersax recordings on Capitol and Columbia.

BENNY CARTER: *The Best of Benny Carter*, Pablo; *In the Mood for Swing* (with Dizzy Gillespie), MusicMasters; *The King*, Pablo; *My Man Benny, My Man Phil* (with Phil Woods), MusicMasters. His historic work from the earlier years is heard on a series of CDs issued by Classics.

BILL CHALLIS: Challis arrangements are to be found in many Paul Whiteman CD reissues. The composition "San," which features Bix Beiderbecke, is one of them. His arrangements for Whiteman include "Dardenella," "Old Man River," "Sweet Sue," and "Let's Do It." For Frank Trumbauer he arranged "Ostrich Walk," and for Fletcher Henderson "Singing the Blues," "Clarinet Marmalade," and "My Gal Sal." These are to be found in various reissue packages. Bassist Vince Giordano organized a big band to make a stereo album of works Challis had written for the Jean Goldkette band. The resulting LP, titled *The Goldkette Project*, can be obtained by writing to Bill's brother, Evan Challis, at P.O. Box 290, Harvey's Lake, Pennsylvania 18618, U.S.A.

JEFF AND JOHN CLAYTON: *The Clayton Brothers*, Concord; *It's All in the Family* (with Roger Kellaway), Concord. John's big-band writing is heard on albums of the Clayton-Hamilton orchestra, including *Groove Shop* and *Heart and Soul*, both on Capri.

DOC CHEATHAM: *Doc Cheatham and Jim Galloway* (with Terry Clarke), Sackville; *Doc Cheatham and Sammy Price*, Sackville; *The Fabulous Doc Cheatham*, Parkwood.

MARC COPLAND: *My Foolish Heart*, Jazz City; *All Blues at Night*, Jazz City; *Tracks*, L&R.

BILL CROW: Bill has never recorded as a leader. He is on records by many artists, but he is heard to particular advantage in some Gerry Mulligan Quartet recordings, and in *Gerry Mulligan and the Concert Jazz Band*, Verve.

JACK DEJOHNETTE: *Jack DeJohnette's Special Edition*, ECM; *The Piano Album*, Landmark. With Keith Jarrett and Gary Peacock: *Standards*, ECM.

HARRY (SWEETS) EDISON: *The Best of Harry Edison*; *For My Friends*; *Simply Sweets*, all on Pablo.

HERB ELLIS: *Roll Call* (with Jake Hanna), Justice; *After You've Gone* (with Sweets Edison), Pablo; *Soft Shoe* (with Sweets Edison), Concord. He is also heard on most of the Oscar Peterson Trio albums of the middle to the late 1950s.

ART FARMER: *The Jazztet* (with Benny Golson), Real Time; *Something to Live For*, Contemporary; *Blame It on My Youth*, Contemporary; *Modern Art* (with Benny Golson), Blue Note.

MAYNARD FERGUSON: *The Birdland Dream Band*, Bluebird; *Chameleon*, Columbia Jazz Contemporary Masters; *Primal Scream*, Columbia; *MF Horn*, CBS; *Blues Roar*, Mobile Fidelity. He also plays on the historic 1954 *Jam Session at EmArcy* album with Max Roach, Harold Land, and Clark Terry.

TOMMY FLANAGAN: *Giant Steps*, Enja; *The Best of Tommy Flanagan*, Pablo; *Tokyo Recital*, Pablo; *Live at Maybeck Recital Hall*, Concord.

LAURIE FRINK: With Gerry Mulligan: *Walk On the Water*, Swing. With Bob Mintzer: *Incredible Journey*, DMP. With David Sanborn: *Upfront*, Elektra.

TERRY GIBBS: *Dream Band* (5 albums); *Terry Gibbs and Buddy DeFranco, Air Mail Special*; *Chicago Fire*, all on Contemporary.

DIZZY GILLESPIE: *The Best of Dizzy Gillespie*, Pablo; *Bird and Diz*, Verve Alpha; *The Legendary Big Band Concerts*, Vogue; *Dizzy Gillespie Meets the Phil Woods Quintet*, Timeless. There is on the Novus label a dazzling album of material he recorded in the mid-1940s, aptly titled *The Bebop Revolution*.

BENNY GOLSON: *Groovin' with Golson*, Fantasy/OJC. With Freddy Hubbard: *Stardust*, Denon. With Art Farmer and the Jazztet: *Back to the City*, Contemporary.

SONNY GREENWICH: *Bird of Paradise*, Justin Time; *Sun Song*, RCI.

AL GREY: *Live at the 1990 Floating Jazz Festival*, Chiaroscuro; *The New Al Grey Quintet*, Chiaroscuro. With J. J. Johnson: *Things Are Getting Better All the Time*, Pablo.

MICHAEL GREY is heard on some recordings with Al Grey.

CHARLIE HADEN: *Quartet West* (with Alan Broadbent and Billy Higgins), Verve; *Quartet West: Haunted Heart*, Verve; *Old and New Dreams*, ECM.

JIM HALL: *Commitment* (with Art Farmer and Tommy Flanagan), Horizon/A&M. With Bill Evans: *Undercurrent*, Blue Note; *Jim Hall and Friends Live at Town Hall* (with Bob Brookmeyer and Gerry Mulligan), MusicMasters. Also with Paul Desmond on *East of the Sun*, Bluebird; and with Ron Carter on *Live at Village West*, Concord.

JAKE HANNA: *Takes Manhattan*; *Jake Hanna and Carl Fontana Live*, both Concord.

ROY HARGROVE: *Diamond in the Rough*; *Public Eye*; *The Vibe*, all on Novus.

THE HARPER BROTHERS: *Artistry*; *Remembrance*; *You Can Hide Inside the Music* (with Ernie Andrews and Sweets Edison), all on Verve.

TOM HARRELL: *Passages*, Chesky; *Sail Away* (with John Abercrombie), Contemporary; *Form* (with Charlie Haden), Contemporary; and a number of recordings by the Phil Woods Quintet, including *Bop Stew*; *Flash*; and *Bouquet*, all on Contemporary.

EDDIE HARRIS: *The Best of Eddie Harris*, Atlantic; *A Tale of Two Cities*, Night; *There Was a Time*, Enja.

JOHN HEARD: There are no albums featuring John as leader. He is on any number of Count Basie albums, including *Satch and Josh Again* (with Oscar Peterson), Pablo; and on Bud Shank's album *That Old Feeling*, Contemporary.

BILLY HIGGINS: *Go!* Blue Note. With Lee Morgan: *The Sidewinder*, Blue Note; *The Soldier* (with Cedar Walton), Timeless.

BILL HOLMAN: *The Bill Holman Band*, JVC; *The Fabulous Bill Holman*, Sackville; *Great Big Band*, Creative World. Stan Kenton recorded a great deal of Holman's work in the mid-1950s, including an album for Capitol entitled *The Music of Bill Holman* and the superb *Contemporary Concepts*. Mosaic has a 4-CD Kenton Package in which Holman is extensively heard.

SHIRLEY HORN. *Close Enough for Love*; *I Thought about You*; *You Won't Forget Me*, all on Verve.

CHUBBY JACKSON: The recordings by Chubby's band are currently out of print. He remain best known for his work with the Woody Herman First Herd, on Columbia.

DUFFY JACKSON: There are at present no available recordings by Jackson as a leader.

CHRISTIAN JACOB: Christian's compositional talent is heard to good effect on the 1987 Gary Burton Quintet release, *Whiz Kids*, ECM.

HANK JONES: *Bluesette*, Black & Blue; *Hank*, All Art Jazz; *The Oracle* (with Billy Higgins), Polydor; *Live at Maybeck Recital Hall*, Concord.

GEOFF KEEZER: *Curveball*, Sunnyside; *Here and Now*, Blue Note. With Art Blakey: *Tippin' In*, Timeless.

ROGER KELLAWAY: *The Roger Kellaway Cello Quartet*, A&M; *Live at Maybeck Recital Hall*, Concord; *In Japan*, All Art Jazz; *Roger Kellaway and Red Mitchell: Dragon*, DRC.

BILL KIRCHNER: *The Bill Kirchner Nonet: Infant Eyes*; *What It Is To Be Frank*, both on Sea Breeze. Arangement of "Tanga" on Dizzy Gillespie's *Live at the Royal Festival Hall*, Enja.

MOE KOFFMAN: *Momentum*; *Moe Koffman Quintet Plays*; *Oo-Papa-Da* (with Dizzy Gillespie), all on Duke Street.

JACKIE (CAIN) AND ROY KRAL: *An Alec Wilder Collection*, Audiophile; *Full Circle*, Contemporary; *One More Rose*; Audiophile.

HAROLD LAND: *Eastward Ho!*, Fantasy; *The Fox*, Fantasy; *Xocia's Dance* (with Billy Higgins), Muse. He is on the Bill Evans' album *Quintessence*, Fantasy.

LOU LEVY: There is far too little of Lou's recent work on records. These are earlier recordings that are available on CD: *Jazz in Four Colors*; *A Most Musical Fella*; and *Unreleased Recording 1954*, all on Fresh Sound. Lou is heard on many of the Supersax recordings.

MUNDELL LOWE: *California Guitar* (with Roger Kellaway), Famous Door; *The Mundell Lowe Quintet*, Fantasy/OJC. He is on a 1990 album titled *Uptown: André Previn with Mundell Lowe and Ray Brown*, Telarc.

BRIAN LYNCH: *In Process*, Ken; *Peer Pressure*, Criss Cross. Lynch is heard on some of the last records of Art Blakey.

ADAM MAKOWICZ: *Naughty Baby*, RCA Novus; *Moonray*, RCA Novus; *The Name Is Makowicz* (with Phil Woods), Sheffield Lab.

HENRY MANCINI: *The Music from Peter Gunn*, RCA; *The Pink Panther* (with Jimmy Rowles on piano), RCA; *The Mancini Touch*, RCA; *Best of the Blues and the Beat*, Fresh Sound.

JOHNNY MANDEL: Records of classic Mandel scores, including *The Sandpiper*; *The Americanization of Emily*; and *Harper*, are hard to find. He contributed extensively to the Natalie Cole *Unforgettable* album on Elektra, and arranged Shirley Horn's *Here's to Life*, Verve.

ALBERT MANGELSDORFF: *Eternal Rhythm*, MPS, *Tromboneliness*, Sackville; *Hot Hut*, EMI-Capitol.

CHRISTIAN MCBRIDE: Christian McBride had not at the time of this writing begun to record as a leader, though there were few musicians in New York as much in demand for sideman assignments. He is heard on the album *Kenny Drew Jr.* (with Winard Harper) on Antilles; Joe Henderson's *Lush Life* on Verve; and Benny Green's *Testifyin': Live at the Village Vanguard* on Blue Note.

ROB MCCONNELL AND THE BOSS BRASS: *Boss Brass & Woods* (with Phil Woods), MCA; *The Brass Is Back*, Concord; *Brassy and Sassy*, Concord. He is heard in a quintet with Ed Bickert and Rick Wilkins on an album titled *Jive 5* on Concord.

JOHN MCNEIL: *I've Got the World on a String*; *The Glass Room*; *Embarkation*, all on SteepleChase.

MARIAN MCPARTLAND: *From This Moment On*; *Live at Maybeck Recital Hall*; *The Benny Carter Songbook*, all on Concord.

CARMEN MCRAE: *Fine and Mellow*, Concord; *You're Lookin' at Me*, Concord; *Sarah: Dedicated to You*, Novus. On the last album, dedicated to Sarah Vaughan, her accompanist is Shirley Horn on piano.

MODERN JAZZ QUARTET: *The Last Concert*, Atlantic; *The Best of the MJQ*, Pablo; *Django*, Fantasy.

GERRY MULLIGAN: *The Best of the Gerry Mulligan Quartet with Chet Baker*, Pacific Jazz; *Gerry Mulligan Meets Ben Webster*, Verve; *Gerry Mulligan and Paul Desmond*, Fantasy; *Walk on the Water*, Swing; *Birth of the Cool*, Blue Note.

ROMANO MUSSOLINI: The pianist has made a number of albums in Italy, but none is currently available in North America.

DICK OATTS: *Brassworks*, DMP; *Dial and Oatts*, DMP. With Red Rodney: *No Turn on Red*, Denon. With the Mel Lewis Sextet: *Lost Art*, MusicMasters.

OSCAR PETERSON: *The Will to Swing*, Verve. This is a two-CD album I edited to cover Oscar's career from 1949 into the 1970s. It is a broad introduction to his work, based on a biography of Oscar that I wrote. Also: *If You Could See Me Now*, Pablo; *Satch and Josh*, Pablo; *The Legendary Oscar Peterson Trio: Saturday Night at the Blue Note* (with Ray Brown and Herb Ellis), Telarc.

CHRIS POTTER: Chris has not yet been widely recorded. He is heard on a Red Rodney album titled *Red Alert*, Continuum.

MEL POWELL: *The Return of Mel Powell*, Chiaroscuro. This is the only jazz recording Powell has made since he played on the Benny Goodman album *B.G. in Hi-Fi*, recorded for Capitol in 1954. Many of Powell's compositions, such as "The Earl" and "Mission to Moscow," and his arrangements are found in Goodman's Columbia recordings from the early 1940s.

ANDRE PREVIN: Like his friend Mel Powell, Previn has not recorded much jazz in the last twenty years. A 1990 album titled *Uptown: André Previn with Mundell Lowe and Ray Brown* is on Telarc, as is *Old Friends*, a more recent release featuring the same players. Many of his earlier albums, however, are still in circulation, among them *André Previn and His Pals*, Fresh Sound; *Like Previn*, Fantasy; *Pal Joey*, Fantasy/OJC.

MAX ROACH: *The Complete Blue Note and Pacific Jazz Recordings of Clifford Brown*, Mosaic; *The Complete EmArcy Recordings of Clifford Brown*, Mosaic; *Paris* (with Dizzy Gillespie), A&M.

CLAUDIO RODITI: *Gemini Man*, Milestone; *Slow Fire*, Milestone; *Two of Swords*, Candid.

RED RODNEY: *Early Be-Bop*, Mercury; *No Turn on Red*, Denon; *Red Alert* (with Chris Potter), Continuum.

SHORTY ROGERS: *Short Stops*, Bluebird; *Swings*, Bluebird; *Yesterday, Today and Tomorrow* (with Bud Shank), Concord.

RENEE ROSNES: *For the Moment*, Blue Note; *Renee Rosnes*, Blue Note.

JIMMY AND STACY ROWLES: *I'm Glad There Is You*; *Looking Back*, both on Delos; *Tell It Like It Is*, Concord.

PETE RUGOLO: Pete made more than twenty albums as a leader; few are now available. Try *Pete Rugolo Plays Kenton*, Mercury; *New Sounds*, Harmony. His best-known work is the writing he did for the Stan Kenton band between 1945 and the early 1950s, available on the Creative World label Kenton founded.

AKIO SASAJIMA: *Som Brasil*, Pausa; *Akio*, Pausa; *Akoustically Sound* (duets with Ron Carter), Muse.

BUD SHANK: *At Jazz Alley*, Contemporary; *Heritage*, Concord; *Tomorrow's Rainbow*, Contemporary.

ARTIE SHAW: *Begin the Beguine*, Bluebird. This is a good introduction to the Shaw band in its peak years. A series of cassettes collectively titled *The Complete Artie Shaw* documents the band from 1938 to 1945. *The Last Recordings*, MusicMasters, catches Shaw in mid-1954 with, among others, Hank Jones.

HORACE SILVER: *The Best of Horace Silver*; *Silver's Blue* (with Donald Byrd); *Song for My Father*, all on Blue Note.

JERI SOUTHERN: Sad to say, Jeri's records are now collectors' items. The usual catalogues do not list one of her records in print in the U.S.A. The album *Coffee, Cigarettes & Memories* has been issued on CD by Fresh Sounds Records of Barcelona, Spain.

BILLY TAYLOR: *Billy Taylor Trio*, Fantasy/OJC; *Cross Section*, Fantasy/OJC; *Taylor Made Jazz*, Fresh Sound.

CLARK TERRY: *Live at the Village Gate* (with Kenny Washington), Chesky; *Portraits*, Chesky; *Serenade to a Bus Seat*, Fantasy/OJC.

EDMUND THIGPEN: *Action-Reaction*, GNP Crescendo; *Young Men & Olds*, Timeless; *Easy Flight*, Reckless Records; *Mr. Taste*, Justin Time, plus the Oscar Peterson Trio records from 1959 to the mid-60s.

DON THOMPSON: *Winter Mist* (playing vibraphone), Jazz Alliance; *Witchcraft* (playing bass and piano), duets with John Abercrombie; *The Ballad Artistry of Buddy Tate* (playing bass), with Ed Bickert and Terry Clarke, Justin Time; *The Brass Is Back* (playing piano) by Rob McConnell and the Boss Brass, Concord.

MCCOY TYNER: *Enlightenment*, Milestone/Fantasy; *3x3* (with John Abercrombie), Milestone/Fantasy; *Tender Moments*, Blue Note. Also many of the recordings of John Coltrane on Impulse.

CEDAR WALTON: *Piano Solos*, Clear Cut; *Cedar* (with Billy Higgins), Fantasy/OJC; *Cedar Walton Plays Cedar Walton* (with Jack DeJohnette and Billy Higgins).

KENNY WASHINGTON: Kenny has made few records as a leader, yet is one of the most recorded drummers of his generation. He is on the Johnny Griffin album *The Cat*, Antilles; Benny Carter's album *All that Jazz* (with Clark Terry), MusicMasters; the Milt Jackson album *The Harem*, MusicMasters; and Ralph Moore's *Furthermore* (with Roy Hargrove), Landmark.

BILL WATROUS: *Best of Bill Watrous*; *Bone Straight Ahead*; *La Zorra*, all on Famous Door.

KENNY WHEELER: *Deer Wan* (with John Abercrombie and Jack DeJohnette); *Gnu High* (with Jack DeJohnette); *The Widow in the Window* (with John Abercrombie); *Music for Large and Small Ensembles*, all on ECM. The last-named shows a too-seldom heard aspect of Wheeler's work, his writing for big band.

RICK WILKINS: With Ed Bickert: *I Wished on the Moon*, Concord. All the Rob McConnell Boss Brass recordings, on various labels. Rick arranged the Oscar Peterson album *The Royal Wedding Suite*, RCA.

SPIEGLE WILLCOX: *The Goldkette Project* (with Bill Challis).

JOE WILLIAMS: *Count Basie Swings, and Joe Williams Sings*, Verve; *In Good Company* (with Shirley Horn), Verve; *Every Night Live at Vine Street*, Verve.

PHIL WOODS: *Birds of a Feather*, Antilles; *Bouquet* (with Tom Harrell), Concord; *Flash* (with Harrell), Concord; *The Rites of Swing*, Candid; *My Man Benny, My Man Phil* (with Benny Carter), MusicMasters.

Index

Author's Acknowledgments

John Reeves and I received an enormous amount of unstinting advice and help in the course of the three years it took to gather this collection of photos and profiles. Constraints of time and availability meant we could not photograph everyone we wanted. I particularly regret that we were unable to get together with J.J. Johnson, the great trombonist.

But I am grateful to those we did manage to see, and to those who made it easier for us. I particularly wish to thank Hank Jones and Jackie and Roy Kral for their hospitality. Above all I thank composer Bill Kirchner, who went far beyond the call of friendship or duty in setting up sittings in the New York City area. He became our co-conspirator, confidant, and social secretary.

I wish particularly to thank John Reeves, who conceived this project and urged it on me. His journey of discovery became my journey of re-discovery, and I viewed afresh the genius of friends whose work I was in danger of taking for granted.

Photographer's Acknowledgments

I will be forever grateful to the boys of my long-gone southern Ontario summers, Michael Hood, Ken Rodmell and Don Sebire, great friends who first led me to jazz, the places to hear jazz and the musicians who played it.

My long-time friend and mentor, the Pennsylvania-based photographer Peter Croydon, along with his wife Zena, facilitated eastern U.S. operations with free accommodation and transport. On one occasion Peter not only did the driving up to Montclair, New Jersey, he also acted as photo-assistant for my Jackie and Roy shoot, an experience that somehow moved him from mild interest in jazz to fanatic fandom.

Share Cameron made my weeks-long visits to southern California both affordable and efficient by providing splendidly packaged bed and breakfast accommodations and crucial helpings of invaluable local knowledge.

My wonderfully talented assistant, Dina Almeida, kept the studio functioning during my long absences, and performed prodigious feats in the darkroom making the hundreds of beautifully crafted enlargements reproduced in *Jazz Lives*.

I will never be able to express sufficient gratitude to my dear friend Joyce Davenall Turner. Joyce's emotional and intellectual support have for years been crucial to every aspect of my life and work. *Jazz Lives* has benefited greatly from her elegant sensibilities and astute critical insights.

216